Praise for Ariel Levy and
Female Chauvinist Pigs

"*New York* magazine writer Ariel Levy strips the 'Girls Gone Wild' culture of its cuteness in her provocative *Female Chauvinist Pigs*, arguing that post-feminist poster girls such as the Playboy Bunnies offer only faux empowerment."
—*Vanity Fair*

"Ariel Levy has become feminism's newest and most provocative voice."
—Cindy Adams, *New York Post*

"Anyone who's shaken his or her head as young women emulate [Paris Hilton] will want to dig into *Pigs* like it's prime rib at a gentlemen's club."
—*New York Post*

"Deeply researched, sparkling with witty outrage, readable."
—*New York Observer*

"Lively, well-reported."
—*The Seattle Times*

"If you've ever wondered how college girls—some of whom must be women's studies majors—can justify participating in wet T-shirt contests or baring their bums for 'Girls Gone Wild' videos, this book offers an explanation. . . . Whip-smart."
—*San Francisco Chronicle*

"Punctuated with a sharp tongue and an even sharper eye, *Female Chauvinist Pigs* is smart, witty, and provocative to read while at the same time alarming."
—*Calgary Herald*

"In *Female Chauvinist Pigs*, Levy takes a sharp-eyed look at perceptions of feminism. [Levy] is a smart, witty observer of American culture."
—*The Miami Herald*

"Culturally astute and not at all preachy."
—*Psychology Today*

"Ariel Levy untangles the contradictions of empowerment. . . . Engaging, smart, and relevant." —*Bust*

"Puts a new, long overdue face on feminism."
—Elle.com

"Well-written social anthropology."
—*The Tampa Tribune*

"A fascinating and furious critique of raunch culture."
—*Library Journal*

"Levy's insightful reporting and analysis chill the hype of what's hot. It will create many 'aha!' moments for readers who have been wondering how porn got to be pop and why 'feminism' is such a dirty word."
—*Publishers Weekly*, starred review

"A piercing look at how women are sabotaging their own attempts to be seen as equals by going about the quest the wrong way. Levy's engrossing book should be required reading for young women."
—*Booklist*, starred review

"[A] biting critique of the phenomenon of raunch culture. . . . An assertive blast, filled with punchy language and vivid images." —*Kirkus Reviews*

"Every once in a while a book takes a cultural trend that's been buzzing around in the background and clarifies it in sharp relief. *Female Chauvinist Pigs* is one of those rare books. This book finally explains some of the stranger pop culture trends of the last few years, from porn becoming cool to college women thinking it's sexy to lift up their shirts. The book also goes beyond explanation to ask what this all means for women and feminism—an enormously relevant question now that women are more powerful than ever yet are expected to be more unclothed than ever. If you want to understand the culture that your daughters and younger sisters are growing up with—and taking for granted—read this book!" —Jean Twenge, author of *Generation Me*

"As everyone knows, we people generally—Americans in particular—let sex drive us mad. *Female Chauvinist Pigs* is a heroic (and smart and entertaining and disturbing) stab at looking very sanely at one rampant form the insanity is taking these days. Ariel Levy understands that while we may defend to death every woman's right to look and act like a whore, it doesn't mean we're prigs if we find it unfortunate."

—Kurt Andersen, author of *Turn of the Century*

"*Female Chauvinist Pigs* is smart, alarming, and extremely funny. With nuance and humor, Levy has written both a convincing exposé of sex and desire in contemporary America and an important cultural history. I'm giving a copy to my mother. And my sons."

—Cathleen Schine, author of *The Love Letter* and *She Is Me*

"Ariel Levy has given us an important, lively, shocking investigative report about how and why—in an age of HIV/AIDS and religious fundamentalism—U.S. commercialism has mainstreamed pornography, popularized raunch images (and practices), and revived female 'bimbo' roles. This is a call to arms for women and girls who are being sold pseudo empowerment, phony liberation, and fake rebellion—instead of the real thing: freedom. A must-read for young women—and everyone else."

—Robin Morgan

"A sharp picture of a culture that is incredibly over-sexualised and yet weirdly unsexy."

—*The Guardian* (London)

"The young U.S. journalist Ariel Levy has done the West a real favour by publishing *Female Chauvinist Pigs*."

—*The Independent* (London)

"Ariel Levy is clever, coherent, and cross, which makes *Female Chauvinist Pigs: Women and the Rise of Raunch Culture* an exciting read."

—*The Daily Telegraph* (London)

Ariel Levy

FEMALE CHAUVINIST PIGS

Women and the Rise of Raunch Culture

Free Press
New York
London
Toronto
Sydney

FREE PRESS
A Division of Simon & Schuster, Inc.
1230 Avenue of the Americas
New York, NY 10020

First Free Press trade paperback edition 2006

FREE PRESS and colophon are trademarks of Simon & Schuster, Inc.

For information about special discounts for bulk purchases, please contact Simon & Schuster Special Sales: 1-800-456-6798 or business@simonandschuster.com

Designed by Karolina Harris

Manufactured in the United States of America
20 19 18 17 16 15 14 13 12

The Library of Congress has catalogued the hardcover edition as follows:
Levy, Ariel.
Female chauvinist pigs: women and the rise of raunch culture/Ariel Levy.
p. cm.
Includes bibliographical references and index.
1. Anti-feminism. 2. Feminism. 3. Sexism. I. Title.
HQ1155 .L48   2005
305.42'0973'090511.—dc22   2005048811
ISBN-13: 978-0-7432-4989-8
ISBN-10:   0-7432-4989-5
ISBN-13: 978-0-7432-8428-8 (Pbk)
ISBN-10:   0-7432-8428-3 (Pbk)

For the two R. L.'s

*What a woman was criticized for doing yes-
terday she is ridiculed for not doing today.*

     — Edith Wharton, 1915

*To name a sensibility, to draw its contours
and to recount its history, requires a deep
sympathy modified by revulsion.*

     — Susan Sontag, 1964

Contents

FEMALE CHAUVINIST PIGS

Introduction

I first noticed it several years ago. I would turn on the television and find strippers in pasties explaining how best to lap dance a man to orgasm. I would flip the channel and see babes in tight, tiny uniforms bouncing up and down on trampolines. Britney Spears was becoming increasingly popular and increasingly unclothed, and her undulating body ultimately became so familiar to me I felt like we used to go out.

Charlie's Angels, the film remake of the quintessential jiggle show, opened at number one in 2000 and made $125 million in theaters nationally, reinvigorating the interest of men and women alike in leggy crime fighting. Its stars, who kept talking about "strong women" and "empowerment," were dressed in alternating soft-porn styles—as massage parlor geishas, dominatrixes, yodeling Heidis in alpine bustiers. (The summer sequel in 2003—in which the Angels' perilous mission required them to perform stripteases—pulled in another $100 million domestically.) In my own industry, magazines, a porny new genre called the Lad Mag, which included titles like *Maxim, FHM,* and *Stuff,* was hitting the stands and becoming a huge success by delivering what *Playboy* had only occasionally managed to capture: greased celebrities in little scraps of fabric humping the floor.

This didn't end when I switched off the radio or the television or closed the magazines. I'd walk down the street and see teens and young women—and the occasional wild fifty-year-old—wearing jeans cut so low they exposed what came to be known as butt cleavage paired with miniature tops that showed off breast implants and pierced navels alike. Sometimes, in case the overall message of the outfit was too subtle, the shirts would be emblazoned with the Playboy bunny or say PORN STAR across the chest.

Some odd things were happening in my social life, too. People I knew (female people) liked going to strip clubs (female strippers). It was sexy and fun, they explained; it was liberating and rebellious. My best friend from college, who used to go to Take Back the Night marches on campus, had become captivated by porn stars. She would point them out to me in music videos and watch their (topless) interviews on *Howard Stern*. As for me, I wasn't going to strip clubs or buying *Hustler* T-shirts, but I was starting to show signs of impact all the same. It had only been a few years since I'd graduated from Wesleyan University, a place where you could pretty much get expelled for saying "girl" instead of "woman," but somewhere along the line I'd started saying "chick." And, like most chicks I knew, I'd taken to wearing thongs.

What was going on? My mother, a shiatsu masseuse who attended weekly women's consciousness-raising groups for twenty-four years, didn't own makeup. My father, whom she met as a student radical at the University of Wisconsin, Madison, in the sixties was a consultant for Planned Parenthood, NARAL, and NOW. Only thirty years (my lifetime) ago, our mothers were "burning their bras" and picketing Playboy, and suddenly we were getting implants and wearing the bunny logo as supposed symbols of our liberation. How had the culture shifted so drastically in such a short period of time?

What was almost more surprising than the change itself were the responses I got when I started interviewing the men and—often—women who edit magazines like *Maxim* and make programs like *The Man Show* and *Girls Gone Wild*. This new raunch culture didn't mark the death of feminism, they told me; it was evidence that the feminist project had already been achieved. We'd *earned* the right to look at *Play-*

boy; we were *empowered* enough to get Brazilian bikini waxes. Women had come so far, I learned, we no longer needed to worry about objectification or misogyny. Instead, it was time for us to join the frat party of pop culture, where men had been enjoying themselves all along. If Male Chauvinist Pigs were men who regarded women as pieces of meat, we would outdo them and be Female Chauvinist Pigs: women who make sex objects of other women and of ourselves.

When I asked female viewers and readers what they got out of raunch culture, I heard similar things about empowering miniskirts and feminist strippers, and so on, but I also heard something else. They wanted to be "one of the guys"; they hoped to be experienced "like a man." Going to strip clubs or talking about porn stars was a way of showing themselves and the men around them that they weren't "prissy little women" or "girly-girls." Besides, they told me, it was all in fun, all tongue-in-cheek, and for me to regard this bacchanal as problematic would be old-school and uncool.

I tried to get with the program, but I could never make the argument add up in my head. How is resurrecting every stereotype of female sexuality that feminism endeavored to banish *good* for women? Why is laboring to look like Pamela Anderson empowering? And how is imitating a stripper or a porn star—a woman whose *job* is to imitate arousal in the first place—going to render us sexually liberated?

Despite the rising power of Evangelical Christianity and the political right in the United States, this trend has only grown more extreme and more pervasive in the years that have passed since I first became aware of it. A tawdry, tarty, cartoonlike version of female sexuality has become so ubiquitous, it no longer seems particular. What we once regarded as a *kind* of sexual expression we now view *as* sexuality. As former adult film star Traci Lords put it to a reporter a few days before her memoir hit the bestseller list in 2003, "When I was in porn, it was like a back-alley thing. Now it's everywhere." Spectacles of naked ladies have moved from seedy side streets to center stage, where everyone—men and women—can watch them in broad daylight. *Playboy* and its ilk are being "embraced by young women in a curious way in a postfeminist world," to borrow the words of Hugh Hefner.

But just because we are post doesn't automatically mean we are feminists. There is a widespread assumption that simply because my generation of women has the good fortune to live in a world touched by the feminist movement, that means everything we do is magically imbued with its agenda. It doesn't work that way. "Raunchy" and "liberated" are not synonyms. It is worth asking ourselves if this bawdy world of boobs and gams we have resurrected reflects how far we've come, or how far we have left to go.

One

RAUNCH
CULTURE

Late on a balmy Friday night in March 2004, a crew from *Girls Gone Wild* sat on the porch of the Chesterfield Hotel on Collins Avenue in Miami, preparing for the night of filming ahead of them. An SUV passed by and two blonde heads popped out of the sunroof like prairie dogs, whooping into the night sky. If you ever watch television when you have insomnia, then you are already familiar with Girls Gone Wild: late at night, infomercials show bleeped-out snippets of the brand's wildly popular, utterly plotless videos, composed entirely from footage of young women flashing their breasts, their buttocks, or occasionally their genitals at the camera, and usually shrieking "Whoo!" while they do it. The videos range slightly in theme, from *Girls Gone Wild on Campus* to *Girls Gone Wild Doggy Style* (hosted by the rapper Snoop Doggy Dogg), but the formula is steady and strong: Bring cameras to amped-up places across the country—Mardi Gras, hard-partying colleges, sports bars, spring break destinations—where young people are drinking themselves batty and offer T-shirts and trucker hats to the girls who flash or the guys who induce them to.

"It's a cultural phenomenon," said Bill Horn, Girls Gone Wild's thirty-two-year-old vice president of communications and marketing, a shaggy-haired young man in a T-shirt and Pumas. "It's like a rite of passage."

A couple of girls with deep tans in tiny, fluttery skirts were chatting across the street from the Chesterfield. "Ladies, throw your hands up!" a guy hollered at them as he passed by. They giggled and complied.

Horn said, "It's the next step."

Girls Gone Wild (GGW) is so popular they are expanding from soft-core videos to launch an apparel line, a compilation CD with Jive Records (of GGW-approved club hits), and a Hooters-like restaurant chain. GGW has a celebrity following: Justin Timberlake has been photographed in a GGW hat, Brad Pitt gave out GGW videos to his *Troy* castmates as wrap presents. And the phrase "Girls Gone Wild" has entered the American vernacular . . . it works well for advertisements (Cars Gone Wild!) and magazine headlines (Curls Gone Wild!).

Puck, a surprisingly polite twenty-four-year-old cameraman, was loading equipment into their van. He wore a GGW hat and T-shirt, which seemed to be enough to draw women to him as if by ensorcellment. Two stunning young women who were already very close to naked asked Puck if they could come along with him if they promised to take off their clothes and make out with each other later for the camera, possibly even in a shower. There was no room for them in the car, but Puck was unconcerned; there would be other such offers. "It's amazing," said GGW's tour manager, Mia Leist, a smiley, guileless, twenty-four-year-old. "People flash for the brand." She pointed at a young woman sitting on the other end of the porch. "Debbie got naked for a hat."

Besides her new GGW hat, nineteen-year-old Debbie Cope was wearing a rhinestone Playboy bunny ring, white stilettos that laced in tight X's up her hairless calves, and wee shorts that left the lowest part of her rear in contact with the night air. Body glitter shimmered across her tan shoulders and rose in a sparkling arc from her cleavage to her clavicle. "The body is such a beautiful thing," she said. "If a woman's got a pretty body and she likes her body, let her show it off! It exudes confidence when people wear little clothes." Cope was a tiny person who could have passed for fifteen. On the preceding night she had done a "scene" for GGW, which is to say she pulled down her shorts and masturbated for them on camera in a hotel room. She said she felt bad for "not doing it right" because for some reason she couldn't achieve orgasm.

"People watch the videos and think the girls in them are real slutty, but I'm a virgin!" Cope said proudly. "And yeah, *Girls Gone Wild* is for guys to get off on, but the women are beautiful and it's . . . fun! The only way I could see someone not doing this is if they were planning a career in politics." Then a song Cope liked came on the radio inside the hotel and she started doing that dance you sometimes see in rap videos, the one where women shake their butts so fast they seem to blur.

"She calls that vibrating," explained Sam, another cameraman. "She told me, 'I can vibrate.'"

"Crazy Debbie," said Mia Leist. "I love her! She gets so many girls for us."

Everyone piled into the van and followed Crazy Debbie to a dance club in nearby Coconut Grove, where she knew all the locals. "Fun girls," Cope promised.

It was a vast, multilevel place and every song had a relentless, throbbing beat. Bill Horn surveyed the scene and landed his eyes on a cluster of blondes in tops tenuously fastened by lots of string ties. "Now *those* are some girls who should go wild," he said. "Jesus, listen to me . . . this job is turning me into a straight guy." Horn, who briefly pursued a career in academia before taking up with GGW, talked about his boyfriend constantly and was the second in command at GGW.

Puck and Sam, the cameramen, passed by with three young women who'd volunteered to do a "private" out on the balcony.

"Here we go," said Horn. He gave a little laugh. "There's some part of me that always wants to shriek, 'Don't do it!'"

But he didn't, and they definitely did . . . the trio started making out in a ravenous lump, grabbing at each other's rears and rutting around while trying to remain upright. Ultimately, one girl fell over and landed giggling on the floor—a characteristic endpoint for a GGW scene.

Later, the girl, her name was Meredith, said she was a graduate student. "It's sad," she said, with only a slight slur. "We'll have Ph.D.s in three years. In anthropology."

A few weeks later, on the telephone, she was upset: "I'm not at all bisexual . . . not that I have anything against that. But when you think about it, I'd never do that *really*. It's more for show. A polite way of putting it is it's like a reflex," she said. "My friend I was with felt really bad, the one who told the first girl to kiss me, the one who started it. Because in the beginning, I felt so dirty about the whole thing. I hate Miami."

"It's a business," said Mia Leist. "In a perfect world, maybe we'd stop and change things. But we know the formula. We know how it works."

"If it gets guys off . . ." said Bill Horn.

"If it gets *girls* off!" Leist interrupted. "It's not like we're creating this. This is happening whether we're here or not. Our founder was just smart enough to capitalize on it." GGW's founder, Joe Francis, has likened the flashing girls he captures on his videos to seventies feminists burning their bras. His product, he says, is sexy for men, liberating for women, good for the goose, and good for the gander. Francis estimates GGW is worth $100 million. He owns a mansion in Bel Air, a retreat in Puerto Vallarta, and two private jets. That weekend in Miami, ABC had just finished shooting a segment on Joe Francis for the show *Life of Luxury.*

GGW may not exactly have bought respectability for Francis: Charges were pending against him for racketeering, although a judge had dismissed charges that he'd offered a girl $50 to touch his penis. ("As if!" Horn shrieked when I asked about it. "As my boyfriend said, when has Joe ever had to pay for a hand job?") But GGW has made Francis rich and fairly famous and certainly a particular kind of L.A. celebrity. His ex-girlfriends include such prize girls gone wild as Paris Hilton and Tara Reid.

Joe Francis didn't come on this particular leg of spring break, but his presence and preferences were felt. The cameramen received bonuses if they captured a hot girl—as opposed to a normal girl—flashing on camera. "Joe's looking for tens," said Leist. "You know, 100 to 110 pounds, big boobs, blonde, blue eyes, ideally no piercing or tattoos." Leist herself was short, with brown hair and a soft chin line. She got her job through one of her professors at Emerson College who had known the previous GGW tour manager. "I've had discussions with friends who were like, 'This is so degrading to females,'" said Leist. "I feel that if you walk up to someone all sly and say, 'Come on, get naked, show me your box,' that's one thing. But if you have women coming up to you *begging* to get on camera and they're having fun and being sexy, then that's another story."

I asked Leist if she would ever appear in a GGW video herself. She said, "Definitely not."

Usually the girls, tens or otherwise, started out joking. They would plead with Puck and Sam to give them GGW hats, and then they'd pretend to peel up their shirts or lift their skirts. But little by little, the tease became the truth, and they took off their clothes as the cameras recorded them for future viewing by God knows who.

Later that night, GGW hit a second bar, part of a chain called Señor Frog's. (It was within walking distance of the Delano Hotel, but minimalism and snobbery felt very far away.) Señor Frog's was having a "sexy positions contest." Two chunky young women with the familiar spring break combination of hair bleached to a radioactive white and skin sunned an angry pink were pretending to hump each other on a raised platform. A group of mostly men circled around them and a rhythmic chant of "TAKE-IT-OFF!

TAKE-IT-OFF!" rose from the crowd. It was followed by a chorus of boos when the women declined to do so, but as a consolation the taller woman poured beer all over the shorter woman's head and breasts.

"Girls! This is not a wet T-shirt contest!" the MC bellowed over the sound system. "Pretend you are fucking! Let me emphasize, pretend you are *really* fucking! I want you to pretend like you're fucking the shit out of her doggy style." The women were too inebriated to achieve sufficient verisimilitude, and the crowd called them offstage.

Mia Leist was suddenly very excited. The bartender had just told her about a "girl-on-girl box-eating" contest in Fort Lauderdale later in the week, which would yield ideal footage for the tapes sold to GGW subscribers, the people who get an explicit video every month for $9.99, as opposed to the occasional buyers who pay $19.99 to purchase a tape of milder content from a GGW infomercial or a Virgin Megastore.

"It's all girl-on-girl, we never shoot guys," explained Bill Horn. "That's not what Joe wants. And no pros. It has to be *real.*"

Reality has always been Joe Francis's beat—specifically, those realities that appeal to people's darkest impulses: voyeurism, violence, and erotomania. On the GGW Web site, you can still purchase Francis's debut effort, *Banned from Television*, a hideous compilation featuring "a public execution, a great white shark attack, a horrifying train accident and an explicit undercover video from a sex club bust!" as the video is described on the site. "That's how Joe made his first million," said Horn.

Out on the back porch, a phalanx of young men watched, entranced, as a very pretty nineteen-year-old from Jupiter, Florida, named Jennifer Cafferty lifted up her pink tube top for the camera. "Okay now, show me your thong," said Puck. She laughed and twirled her honey-colored hair around her forefinger. "Just show me your thong," he said again. "Just really quick. Just show me your thong. Show me your thong now." She whipped around and lifted her skirt.

"Yeah," shrieked one of the young men watching her. "Yeah, yeah!"

Then she put her hands on her hips and said, "Where's my hat?"

The next day at the beach, only the light was different. "We want our picture with you!" a blonde in a bikini yelled at the crew, shaking her digital camera in the air.

"We don't want pictures," Leist called back. "We want boobs!"

"I think I'm going to have that embroidered on a pillow," said Horn.

A pack of guys were drinking beer out of a funnel, and they decided they wanted GGW hats. Badly.

"Show them your tits," one yelled at the two girls splayed on towels next to him. "What's your problem? Just show them your tits."

Puck set up the shot and waited with his camera

poised for the female response. "No way!" the girl in the black bikini said, pouting.

"You know you want to," the funnel-wielder taunted. People started to circle around, like seagulls sensing a family about to abandon their lunch. "Do it," the guy said.

"Yeah, do it!" yelled a spectator.

"Show your tits!" screamed another.

"Show your ass!"

There were maybe forty people now gathered in a circle that was simultaneously tightening inward and expanding outward around Puck and the girls and their "friends" with every passing second. The noise rose in volume and pitch.

I caught myself hoping the crowd would not start throwing rocks at the girls if they decided to keep their clothes on.

We'll never know, because after a few more minutes passed and a few more dozen dudes joined the massive amoeba of people hollering and standing on top of beach chairs and climbing up on each other's shoulders to get a good view of what might happen, it happened. The girl pulled down her black bathing suit bottom and was rewarded by an echoing round of shrieks that sliced the sky.

"More!" someone yelled.

Other people pulled out their cameras. The people who had cameras built into their cell phones flipped them open and jumped up to try to get shots of the action over the human wall.

The second girl rose up off her towel, listened to the cheers for a moment, and then spanked her friend to the rhythm of the hooting.

"Yo," a guy said into his phone. "This is the best beach day ever."

It sounds like a fantasy world dreamed up by teenage boys. A world of sun and sand where frozen daiquiris flow from faucets and any hot girl you see will peel off her bikini top, lift up her skirt . . . all you have to do is ask. It's no surprise that there's a male audience for this, but what's strange is that the women who populate this alternate reality are not strippers or paid performers, they are middle-class college kids on vacation—they are mainstream. And really, their reality is not all that unusual. People on spring break are obviously young, and Horn was right to call the flashing a rite of passage. But it is an initiation into something ongoing rather than a one-shot deal, more like having a first beer than a bat mitzvah. The heat is turned up a little in Miami, but a baseline expectation that women will be constantly exploding in little blasts of exhibitionism runs throughout our culture. Girls Gone Wild is not extraordinary, it's emblematic.

If you leave your house or watch television you probably already know what I'm talking about, but let's review some examples:

• Jenna Jameson, the world's highest grossing adult film performer, is her own industry. She has been in music videos for Eminem and Korn and advertisements for Pony and Abercrombie & Fitch (a brand whose target market is teenagers). She has taped voice-over for the video game Grand Theft Auto. She was on the best-seller list for six weeks in 2004 with her memoir *How to Make Love Like a Porn Star*, which was written up in the *Philadelphia Inquirer*, the *San Francisco Chronicle*, the *New York Times*, the *Los Angeles Times*, and *Publishers Weekly*. There was something profoundly weird about the fact that one of the most widely read authors in the country was simultaneously selling "ultra-realistic, life-like" replicas of "Jenna's Vagina and Ass" with complimentary lubricant on her own Web site.

In 2003, there was a massive, four-story billboard of Jameson hovering above Times Square. The group Women Against Pornography used to give tours of the area in the late 1970s, when Times Square was a seedy red-light ghetto, in the hopes that "radical feminists, with our deeper understanding of porn and our sophisticated knowledge of sexuality, would succeed in turning around public opinion where old-fashioned moralists had not," as the feminist Susan Brownmiller wrote in *In Our Time: Memoir of a Revolution*. It didn't work, but decades later, developers, chain stores, and Disney succeeded where the feminists had failed and the neighborhood became the spit-shined shopping smorgasbord it is today—a suitable destination for red tour buses with guides far less invested in overthrowing the patriarchy than Susan Brownmiller was. Now that porn stars are no less mainstream or profitable than Mickey Mouse, however, a giant billboard of Jameson—the star of movies like *Philmore Butts* and *Up and Cummers*—is perfectly at home at the Crossroads of the World.

In 2005, Jameson's publisher, Judith Regan, told CBS, "I believe that there is a porno-ization of the culture . . . what that means is that if you watch every single thing that's going on out there in the popular culture, you will see females scantily clad, implanted, dressed up like hookers, porn stars and so on, and that this is very acceptable."

• Female Olympic athletes took time out from their rigorous training schedules in the weeks before the summer 2004 games in Athens to appear naked in *Playboy,* or next to naked in *FHM (For Him Magazine).* There was high-jumper Amy Acuff laying on the ground—her blonde hair pooled around her, eyes closed, hips thrust skyward—in *FHM* (pages away from a sex quiz that included the question "Have you ever participated in a gang bang?" and the answer "Why else do you think my parents shelled out more than $100,000 for college?"). A few pages later, Amanda Beard, the world record–holder in the two-hundred-meter breast stroke, knelt with legs spread and lips parted while she used one hand to hike her top up and expose the underside of her breasts, and the other to pull her bikini bottom down low enough on her pubic bone to prove to the world that she was thoroughly waxed. Haley Clark, a former world record–holder in the one-hundred-meter backstroke and world championship gold medalist, was pictured naked and bending over in *Playboy*, in a position referred to as "presenting" when exhibited in the animal kingdom. The collective effect of these pictures of hot (and, in most cases, wet) girls with thighs parted, tiny, porny patches of pubic hair, and coy, naughty-girl pouts made it almost impossible to keep sight of the women's awesome physical gifts. But then, that may have been the whole point: Bimbos enjoy a higher standing in our culture than Olympians right now. Perhaps the athletes felt they were trading up.

• Lesser jocks are striving for their own red-light experience. "Cardio Striptease" classes are now offered at Crunch gyms in New York, Los Angeles, Miami, San Francisco, and Chicago. "Strong, powerful women are sharing it," Los Angeles instructor Jeff Costa told me. These strong, powerful women are encouraged to attend their workout sessions in bras and thongs to add frisson to the fantasy that they are *real strippers*, who have mysteriously come to symbolize sexual liberation despite the fact that it is their job to *fake* arousal. "Stripping equals sex!" Costa said. "Look at music videos, Victoria's Secret ads, all this stuff . . . lap dancing is everywhere! Ask anyone doing choreography right now: This is where it's at." Costa proudly told me that a mother had recently brought her daughter and eight of the girl's friends to one of his classes for a sweet sixteen celebration.

• ABC aired the first televised Victoria's Secret fashion show in 2001. "Security is tight, and so are the girls!" quipped host Rupert Everett. It was a cavalcade of legs and breasts interspersed with centerfoldish interviews with the models—one aspired to fly to the moon, another loved animals. At first, people were surprised and a little rattled to see soft-core on network television during prime time. But a panty procession would soon seem quaint, compared to the tidal wave of reality shows that swept over television and brought our culture that much closer to a raunch aesthetic and state of mind.

Harem-themed reality shows were particularly successful. In *The Bachelor, Who Wants to Marry a Millionaire?, Joe Millionaire,* and *Outback Jack,* troupes of women were secluded with one man in various bodice-ripper fantasy locales, like a castle or a McMansion or the wilds of Australia. There the women engaged in competitions, many of which involved bikinis, to show who among them was the hottest and the hungriest. Contestants for the hunk spoke with fetishistic longing about getting married and, more importantly, about their fantasy weddings before they'd ever met the groom. A contestant on

The Bachelor gave a proud soliloquy on the yards of white silk she'd already purchased for her wedding gown; another spoke about wanting to find her "Prince Charming" so she could "feel like a real woman."

The reality TV universe is a place that seems strangely untouched by any significant cultural event of the twentieth century, least of all the feminist movement. Even NBC's smash *The Apprentice,* a show that supposedly hinges on the financial acumen and professional cunning of America's future business leaders as assessed by Donald Trump, culminated its first season in a thonged flurry of exhibitionism when four of the show's female cast members appeared in their underwear in the May 2004 issue of *FHM.* For free. As Trump put it to Larry King, they "did this for nothing. Perhaps that's why they didn't win the contest."

• Between 1992 and 2004, breast augmentation procedures in this country went from 32,607 a year to 264,041 a year—that's an increase of more than 700 percent. "The younger girls think that beauty is raised cheeks, a higher brow, big breasts and fuller lips— you know Pam Anderson," Dr. Terry Dubrow told the *New York Times.* Dubrow was one of the two plastic surgeons responsible for the gory, cookie-cutter makeovers on *The Swan,* a reality series launched on Fox in 2004 in which average-looking women were surgically, cosmetically, and sartorially redone to look average in a shinier, pornier way—the brunettes became blondes, the breasts became bigger, the clothes got tighter and sparklier, and all the teeth became implausibly white.

Local newspapers like LA Weekly carry page after page of ads for surgeons who specialize in "vaginoplasty" or "vaginal rejuvenation." That is: cosmetic operations to alter the labia and vulva so they look more like the genitals one sees in Playboy or porn. The surgeries are not intended to enhance sexual pleasure. They are designed exclusively to render a vagina "attractive." The Society of Gynecologic Surgeons has warned that vaginoplasties can cause painful scarring and nerve damage that impede sexual function (i.e., make the vulva painfully hypersensitive or numb), but nevertheless the demand for these procedures is increasing. On plasticsurgerybeverlyhills.net it says "plastic surgery of the vulva has become quite popular over the past 5–8 years," and is "being considered by women of all ages." They caution that large labia "can give a ragged appearance" to the female nether regions if they aren't "corrected."

• The spring 2004 fashion shows oozed so much smut they prompted Barneys Creative Director Simon Doonan to write in his New York Observer column, "The hetero porno antics which dominated the first few days of Fashion Week were a mystery to us attendees . . . we poofters and fashion chicks, when confronted with all this Bada Bing muff culture, can only stare at each other like terrified gerbils trapped in the headlights." The designer Jeremy Scott decorated his show (which he called "Sexybition") with pole dancers and the actress Lisa Marie, who was dressed as a dungeon sex slave and appeared to be having either an extended orgasm or an epileptic seizure onstage. Likewise, the Pierrot knitwear show was set up like a mock porno shoot with the designer, Pierre Carrilero, playing the director and the models rolling around in various familiar porn tableaux (black man/white woman, three-way, etc.). Designer Betsey Johnson's tagline was "Guys Love B.J.," and to enhance her message Johnson's models wore labels like "Fluffer" down the runway. (A fluffer is a person on a porn set whose job is to keep the male performer's penis erect.)

• Elton John, a knighted performer known for queenie costumes, giant wigs, and of late, treacly compositions for animated Disney movies, set his stage for a series of gigs in Las Vegas in the spring of 2004 with a pair of enormous inflatable breasts in front of a massive LED screen on which he played a film of Pamela Anderson spinning around a pole. The huge shows were held at the 4,100-capacity Colosseum at Caesars Palace. Despite his popularity with royalty, children, and gay men, John's concert had the look and feel of a very large Hooters club.

• In publishing, recent years have seen a spate

of X-rated books—none of which have been sheepishly tucked away in the Erotica section behind the Kama Sutra. *XXX: 30 Porn-Star Portraits*, a collection of photos by the prominent photographer Timothy Greenfield-Sanders, came out in October 2004 with accompanying essays by big-name writers like Gore Vidal and Salman Rushdie. The portraits were sold at the famous Mary Boone Gallery in New York City. At the opening of the show, I asked Greenfield-Sanders—whose former subjects have included Supreme Court Justice Ruth Bader Ginsburg, Senator Hillary Clinton, and former Secretary of State Madeleine Albright—why he chose to move from politicians to porn stars. "Because porn has become so much more a part of our culture," he said.

Pamela Anderson's autobiographical novel, *Star*, which came with a nude pinup of the author on the reverse side of the book jacket, stayed on the *New York Times* best-seller list for two weeks in the summer of 2004. Back when hooker-turned-writer Tracy Quan's *Diary of a Manhattan Call Girl* came out in 2001, you could find it prominently displayed at Barnes & Noble, right next to *Harry Potter*. Quan shared a "Meet the Author" event in Washington, D.C., with Chief Justice William Rehnquist. As she put it to the *New York Times*, "If that's not being part of the Establishment, I don't know what is."

● ● ●

This is our establishment, these are our role models, this is high fashion and low culture, this is athletics and politics, this is television and publishing and pop music and medicine and—good news!— being a part of it makes you a strong, powerful woman. Because we have determined that all empowered women must be overtly and publicly sexual, and because the only sign of sexuality we seem to be able to recognize is a direct allusion to red-light entertainment, we have laced the sleazy energy and aesthetic of a topless club or a *Penthouse* shoot throughout our entire culture.

This comes from an article that ran in the *Washington Post* . . . not exactly a fringe publication:

> Who hasn't dreamed of doing a fireman spin around a stripper pole? Because over-the-knee boots are an uptown girl's way of getting down. Because Carmen Electra—star of a new striptease-for-exercise DVD series—is eager to teach America's women how to play a "naughty secretary." Because Madonna pole-dances in a magazine and Kate Moss pole-dances in a video and Pamela Anderson once talked of quitting acting to strip during Kid Rock's concerts. Because Oprah recently learned how to do a stripper walk. Because stripping will tone your abs or heal your soul . . . Because it's hot and men like it. Because it's powerful; forget the men. All this is why everybody wants to be a stripper. It's

why these days the stripper pole—which you
can buy cheap online and install in your den—
seems to run like a steel beam of sleaze through
the American psyche. With stripper-chic, as with
so many advances in popular culture, the nation
owes a great debt to Los Angeles.

One wonders how we will ever be able to repay Los
Angeles for this powerful, soul-healing advance.
"Everybody" wants in on this; "who hasn't dreamed"
of it? We skipped over the part where we just accept
and respect that *some* women like to seem exhibition-
istic and lickerish, and decided instead that *everyone*
who is sexually liberated ought to be imitating strippers and porn stars.

Not so long ago, the revelation that a woman in
the public eye had appeared in any kind of pornography would have destroyed her image. Think of
Vanessa Williams, crowned the first black Miss America in 1983, and how quickly she was dethroned after
her nude photos surfaced in *Penthouse*. Later she
made a comeback as a singer, but the point is that
then, being exposed in porn was something you
needed to come back from. Now, being in porn is itself the comeback.

You may remember that Paris Hilton was but a
blonde teenager with a taste for table-dancing and a
reported $28 million inheritance with her name on it
when she and former boyfriend Rick Solomon made
a video of themselves having sex. Coincidentally or

not, the tape got out and became a staple on Internet porn sites a few years later, right before Hilton's reality series, *The Simple Life,* debuted on Fox in December 2003. In September 2004 a second tape of Hilton having sex, this time with Nick Carter, a former member of the band Backstreet Boys, and Jason Shaw, a Tommy Hilfiger model, started making the rounds. The point, though, is not what she did, but what *we* did with it. The net result of these adventures in amateur pornography was that Paris Hilton became one of the most recognizable and marketable female celebrities in the country. Since the advent of the sex tapes, Hilton has become famous enough to warrant a slew of endorsement deals . . . there is a Paris Hilton jewelry line (belly-button rings feature prominently); a perfume; a string of nightclubs called Club Paris set to open in New York, Atlanta, Madrid, Miami, Las Vegas, London, and Paris; and a modeling contract for Guess jeans that has landed Hilton all over the pages of *Vogue, Lucky,* and *Vanity Fair.* Her book, *Confessions of an Heiress,* was a best-seller in the summer of 2004. Her debut CD—the first single is entitled "Screwed"—is forthcoming. And at the close of 2004, Barbara Walters interviewed the heiress as part of her annual special on the ten "most fascinating people" of the year. Paris Hilton isn't some disgraced exile of our society. On the contrary, she is our mascot.

This may seem confusing considering the "swing to the right" this country has taken, but raunch culture transcends elections. The values people vote for are not necessarily the same values they live by. No region of the United States has a higher divorce rate than the Bible Belt. (The divorce rate in these southern states is roughly fifty percent above the national average.) In fact, eight of the ten states that lead in national divorce are red, whereas the state with the lowest divorce rate in the country is deep blue Massachusetts. Even if people consider themselves conservative or vote Republican, their political ideals may be just that: a reflection of the way they *wish* things were in America, rather than a product of the way they actually experience it.

This is apparent in entertainment as well. During the month that sanctity-of-marriage–touting George W. Bush was elected to his second term in the White House, the second-highest-rated show on television was ABC's *Desperate Housewives,* a cleavage-heavy drama featuring a married woman who sleeps with her teenage gardener. In the conservative greater Atlanta market, for instance, where nearly 58 percent of voters cast their ballot for Bush, *Desperate Housewives* was the number one show. *Playboy* is likewise far more popular in conservative Wyoming than in liberal New York.

If the rise of raunch seems counterintuitive because we hear so much about being in a conservative moment, it actually makes perfect sense when we think about it. Raunch culture is not essentially progressive, it is essentially commercial. By going to strip clubs and flashing on spring break and ogling our Olympians in *Playboy*, it's not as though we are embracing something liberal—this isn't Free Love. Raunch culture isn't about opening our minds to the possibilities and mysteries of sexuality. It's about endlessly reiterating one particular—and particularly commercial—shorthand for sexiness.

There is a disconnect between sexiness or hotness and sex itself. As Paris Hilton, the breathing embodiment of our current, prurient, collective fixations—blondeness, hotness, richness, anti-intellectualism—told *Rolling Stone* reporter Vanessa Grigoriadis, "my boyfriends always tell me I'm not sexual. Sexy, but not sexual." Any fourteen-year-old who has downloaded her sex tapes can tell you that Hilton looks excited when she is posing for the camera, bored when she is engaged in actual sex. (In one tape, Hilton took a cell phone call during intercourse.) She is the perfect sexual celebrity for this moment, because our interest is in the appearance of sexiness, not the existence of sexual pleasure. (Before Paris Hilton we had Britney Spears and Jessica Simpson to drool over: two shiny, waxy blondes who used to tell us over and over again that sex was something they sang about, not something they actually engaged in.)

Sex appeal has become a synecdoche for all appeal: People refer to a new restaurant or job as "sexy" when they mean hip or powerful. A U.S. Army general was quoted in *The New Yorker* regarding an air raid on the Taliban as saying "it was sexy stuff," for instance; the *New York Times* ran a piece on the energy industry subheadlined "After Enron, Deregulation Is Looking Less Sexy." For something to be noteworthy it must be "sexy." Sexiness is no longer just about being arousing or alluring, it's about being worthwhile.

Passion isn't the point. The glossy, overheated thumping of sexuality in our culture is less about connection than consumption. Hotness has become our cultural currency, and a lot of people spend a lot of time and a lot of regular, green currency trying to acquire it. Hotness is not the same thing as beauty, which has been valued throughout history. Hot can mean popular. Hot can mean talked about. But when it pertains to women, hot means two things in particular: fuckable and salable. The literal job criteria for our role models, the stars of the sex industry.

And so sex work is frequently and specifically referenced by the style or speech or creative output of women in general. Consider the oeuvre of pop singer Christina Aguilera, who titled her 2003 album *Stripped* (the tour was sold out and pulled in $32 million), mud-wrestled in a humping fashion in her video *Dirrty,* and likes to wear assless chaps. "She's a wonderful role model," Aguilera's mother proclaimed on a VH1 special about her daughter, "trying to change society so that a woman can do whatever men do."

It is true that women are catching up with men

in the historically masculine department of sexual opportunism; trying to get the best and the most for ourselves in that arena as we are everywhere else. But it's not true that men parade around in their skivvies as a means to attaining power, at least not men in mainstream heterosexual American culture—they don't have to. Jay Leno sits floppy faced and chunky in a loose suit behind his desk, confident that he is the king of late night. When Katie Couric guest-hosted the *Tonight Show* in May 2003, she wore a low-cut dress and felt the need to emphasize her breasts by pointing at them and proclaiming "these are actually real!" Lest the leg men in the house feel understimulated, Couric also had guys with power tools cut a hole in Leno's desk so that the program could be a more complete peep show—a Google search for "Katie Couric legs" provides links to dozens of porn sites with her calves in close-up, in case you missed it. Even America's morning TV sweetheart, a woman who interviews heads of state and is the highest paid *person* in television news—outearning Ted Koppel, Tom Brokaw, Peter Jennings, Mike Wallace, and her cohost Matt Lauer with her $65 million contract—has to dabble in exhibitionism to feel as though she's really made it today.

Couric later commented that she wanted to show America her "fun" side on the *Tonight Show,* but in truth she was exposing more than being fun, or even being sexual. Really what she was showing was that she was open to a certain sort of attention—

which is something that we specifically require if we are going to think of a woman as hot. Hotness doesn't just *yield* approval. Proof that a woman actively *seeks* approval is a crucial criterion for hotness in the first place.

For women, and only for women, hotness requires projecting a kind of eagerness, offering a promise that any attention you receive for your physicality is welcome. When Leno did his stint at Couric's post on the *Today Show*, he remained fully clothed. While Janet Jackson introduced Americans to her right nipple at the notorious 2004 Super Bowl half-time show, Justin Timberlake's wardrobe managed not to malfunction. Not one male Olympian has found it necessary to show us his penis in the pages of a magazine. Proving that you are hot, worthy of lust, and—necessarily—that you seek to provoke lust is still exclusively women's work. It is not enough to be successful, rich, and accomplished: Even women like Couric and Jackson and world-champion swimmer Haley Clark, women at the pinnacle of their fields, feel compelled to display their solicitude. As that girl gone wild put it, this has become "like a reflex."

This is not a situation foisted upon women. Because of the feminist movement, women today have staggeringly different opportunities and expectations than our mothers did. We have attained a degree of hard-won (and still threatened) freedom in our personal lives. We are gradually penetrating the highest levels of the work force. We get to go to college and play sports and be secretary of state. But to look around, you'd think all any of us want to do is rip off our clothes and shake it.

Some version of a sexy, scantily clad temptress has been around through the ages, and there has always been a demand for smut. But this was once a guilty pleasure on the margins—on the almost entirely male margins. For a trend to penetrate political life, the music industry, art, fashion, and taste the way raunch culture has, it must be thoroughly mainstream, and half that mainstream is female. Both men and women alike seem to have developed a taste for kitschy, slutty stereotypes of female sexuality resurrected from an era not quite gone by. We don't even think about it anymore, we just expect to see women flashing and stripping and groaning everywhere we look.

If men have been appreciating the village belly dancer or the Champagne Room lap dancer for sexual gratification and titillation over the years, we have to wonder what women are getting out of this now. Why would a straight woman want to see another woman in fewer clothes spin around a pole? Why would she want to be on that pole herself? Partly, because women in America don't want to be excluded from anything anymore: not the board meeting or the cigar that follows it or, lately, even the trip to the strip club that follows that. What we want is to be where it's at, and currently that's a pretty trashy place.

It no longer makes sense to blame men. Mia Leist and plenty of other women are behind the scenes, not just in front of the cameras, making decisions, making money, and hollering "We want boobs." Playboy is a case in point. Playboy's image has everything to do with its pajama-clad, septuagenarian, babe-magnet founder, Hugh Hefner, and the surreal world of celebrities, multiple "girlfriends," and nonstop bikini parties he's set up around himself. But in actuality, Playboy is a company largely run by women. Hefner's daughter Christie is the chairman and CEO of Playboy Enterprises. The CFO is a middle-aged mother named Linda Havard. The Playboy Foundation (which has supported the ERA and abortion rights, among other progressive causes) is run by Cleo Wilson, an African-American former civil rights activist. A woman named Marilyn Grabowski produces more than half the magazine's photo features.

The company, which celebrated its fiftieth anniversary in 2003, is valued at $465 million; their brand and bunny are ubiquitous; they recently and successfully moved into the televised soft-core porn market; *Playboy* remains the world's top-selling men's magazine, with a paid circulation of just over three million in the United States and some fifteen million readers across the globe. And, after twenty years in remission, the first of many new Playboy Clubs is set to open at the Palms Casino in Las Vegas in 2006. Like the original swinging sixties Playboy Clubs, the new ones will be staffed by "hostesses" dressed in strapless bathing suit–like uniforms topped off with rabbit ears, shirt cuffs, and bunny tails—the same conceit that prompted Gloria Steinem to go under-cover at a Playboy Club in Manhattan for two weeks in 1963 to write her famous article "A Bunny's Tale," in which she seared the women's working conditions and pronounced the club's atmosphere generally con-ducive to exploitation and misogyny. (Steinem's as-sessment was refuted, much less famously, by former bunny Kathryn Leigh Scott in a book called *The Bunny Years.* Scott, who worked alongside Steinem in Manhattan, recollected the Playboy Club chiefly as a pleasant place where she made a lot of money.) Play-boy closed the last of the original clubs in 1986 be-cause they were no longer profitable, but now with the country's reinvigorated interest in all things bimbo, Playboy has determined, probably correctly, that the time is again right to offer Americans cock-tails served by women dressed as stuffed animals.

Christie Hefner is a founder of two women's groups: Emily's List, which raises money to support pro-choice, female Democratic political candidates, and the Committee of 200, an organization of female executives and business owners who provide mentor-ing programs and scholarships to young women and girls. I wanted to find out how she reconciled the work she does for women's advancement with her job as head of a company that uses women as decorative inducements to masturbate, so I went to visit her in Chicago during the city's green, rainy spring.

There was no hint of debauchery in the lobby at 680 North Lake Shore Drive, the building that houses Playboy Enterprises. The floor was a giant chessboard of cool marble, and an understated stainless steel sign spelled out the company's name. (No bunny.) But when I stepped on the elevator, I knew I was in the right place. A tall, rock-hard woman in jeans and heels with a long, silky ponytail and a motherlode of cleavage got on with her friend, who looked more garden-variety blonde human female. The hot one applied another layer of lip gloss, licked her white teeth, and then bared them. "How do I look?" she asked. Her friend scrutinized her with great concentration and then pulled the zipper of her tight terry cloth top down an inch from the midpoint to the base of her cleavage. She stepped back, surveyed her work, and nodded. "I think that's more what you want to say."

On the fifteenth floor, a blonde receptionist was sitting in front of a glass case that housed two weird, white, rabbit-headed mannequins. "Are you all here for the fiftieth?" she asked, smiling. She meant: Were we going to audition to be Playmates in the fiftieth-anniversary issue of the magazine? The one of us who obviously *was* followed the receptionist back into the belly of the building. "She works for a German pharmaceutical company called BrainLAB," her friend told me as she flipped through a copy of the magazine she'd picked up off the coffee table. A few moments passed and then she looked up from a spread on college girls, wild eyed. "I'm going too," she said. "What the hell!" Then she went dashing in after them.

There was a sharp difference in aesthetic and attitude between the women in the lobby and the woman I was there to see. The Playboy offices are designed as glass fishbowls that you can see inside of when you approach from the stairs, so you can watch Christie Hefner long before you actually meet her. She has good skin and a short French manicure and she looks quite a bit like the actress Jo Beth Williams . . . you want to find Hef in her face, but he just isn't there. "You know I used to laugh when people would ask, 'How can you be CEO of a company whose products are sold to men?'" she said, smiling. "I said, gee, it never seemed to occur to people to ask that question all those years when all the *women's* fashion and cosmetic and everything else companies were run by *men!* Nobody sat around going, well, how would *he* know whether this would appeal to women?"

Actually, more than a hundred women literally did sit around on the floor of *Ladies' Home Journal* editor-in-chief John Mack Carter's office for eleven hours on March 18, 1970, with a list of "nonnegotiable demands" like "We demand that the *Ladies' Home Journal* hire a woman editor-in-chief who is in touch with women's real problems and needs." But in any case, I wasn't there to question Hefner's ability to produce a product that appeals to men; the numbers show she can deliver that. I was there to hear about what Playboy does for women.

"A lot of women read the magazine," she said. "We know they read it because we get letters from them." And this was proof, she said, that the "post–sexual revolution, post–women's movement generation that is now out there in their late twenties and early thirties—and then it continues with the generation behind them, too—has just a more grown-up, comfortable, *natural* attitude about sex and sexiness that is more in line with where guys were a couple generations before. The rabbit head symbolizes sexy fun, a little bit of rebelliousness, the same way a navel ring does . . . or low-rider jeans! It's an obvious *I'm taking control of how I look and the statement I'm making* as opposed to *I'm embarrassed about it* or *I'm uncomfortable with it*. A little bit of that in-your-face . . . but in a *fun* way . . . 'frisky' is a good word."

I asked her why she supposed all these frisky, in-your-face women were buying *Playboy* instead of, say, *Playgirl*. "To say that the gap is closing isn't to say that the gap has closed," she replied. "You can't put male nudity on the screen and get an R rating; you can't put male nudity in an ad the way you can put female nudity in an ad and have it be perfectly acceptable. I mean, we still have a disconnect because of the attitude that men have about being uncomfortable with being the objects of women's fantasies and gaze."

That would explain why men would be less likely than women to dream about one day appearing in the pages of *Playgirl.* (Why there aren't any men charging out of the lobby and into the photo shoots saying, *What the hell! It's worth a shot!*) But it doesn't explain why women would be buying the magazine, the rabbit head merchandise . . . the shtick. I think that has more to do with the current accepted wisdom that Hefner articulated so precisely: The only alternative to enjoying *Playboy* (or flashing for *Girls Gone Wild* or getting implants or reading Jenna Jameson's memoir) is being "uncomfortable" with and "embarrassed" about your sexuality. Raunch culture, then, isn't an entertainment option, it's a litmus test of female uptightness.

I asked Hefner how she felt about young girls aspiring to be in *Playboy*—girls like the ones she provides scholarships to through the Committee of 200. "The reason why I think it's perfectly okay is because the way women see being in the magazine is not as a career but as a statement," she said firmly. "It's a moment that lets them be creative. That can be as simple as *I just want to feel attractive,* or it can be very complicated, as has happened with a Vicky La Motta or a Joan Collins, saying, *I am older and I want to reassert the ability to be attractive now that I'm fifty.* Or: *I'm an athlete and I don't think athleticism in women is at odds with being sexy.* It can be something as profound as [a woman] who had a car accident in her twenties and was a paraplegic and wrote us a letter wanting to be in the magazine and tell her story. So I think people who choose to pose for the magazine have a very definite idea of what they want to get out of it—and then they have a life and they may be an actress or a mother or a lawyer or an executive."

An actress or a mother sure, but a lawyer or an executive not necessarily. Putting your tush on display is still not the best way to make partner or impress the board. The only career for which appearing in *Playboy* is a truly strategic move is a career in the sex industry. In *How to Make Love Like a Porn Star,* Jenna Jameson writes, "Beginning with nude modeling is a nice way to ease into it." Many women who appear in Internet or home video porn were "discovered" in *Playboy.* Playboy discourages this practice, and several former Playmates have been barred from the mansion after breaking the unofficial rule against appearing in pornography (never mind the fact that Playboy itself operates the soft-core Spice television network). Still, porn directors continue to use *Playboy* and *Penthouse* as casting catalogues. Women who appeared in *Playboy* have also been recruited to be live-in hookers in the Sultan of Brunei's brother's harem.

The more basic way *Playboy* undermines the female sexual liberation Hefner claims to promote is this: The women who do go into careers outside the sex industry will never be seen by the millions of men—and the growing number of women—who read *Playboy* as actresses or mothers or lawyers or executives; they will never be seen as themselves. They will only ever be seen spread out, in soft focus, wearing something slight and fluffy and smiling in that gentle, wet-lipped way that suggests they will be happy to take whatever is given to them. They are expressing that they are sexy only if sexy means obliging and well paid. If sexy means passionate or invested in one's own fantasies and sexual proclivities, then the pictorials don't quite do it. A model named Alex Arden, a former *Penthouse* cover girl, told interviewers from VH1:

> When you get yourself into the really contortionist position that you've got to hold up and your back hurts and you've got to suck in your stomach, you've got to stick your hips out, you've got to arch your back and you've got to stick your butt out all at the same time and suck in and hold your breath, you don't feel sexy. You feel pain. And you feel like you want to kill [the photographer].

The well-known nudie photographer Earl Miller, for his part, said, "Our job is to go out and bring 'em back alive or dead or whatever . . . we gotta get the picture." Porn queen Jenna Jameson echoed Arden's sentiment when she wrote about her early test shoots for mainstream men's magazines: "I had to arch so hard that my lower back cramped. When I see those photos now, it seems obvious that sexy pout I thought I was giving the camera was just a poorly disguised grimace of pain."

Doesn't sound like something you would do for fun. There are some women who are probably genuinely aroused by the idea or the reality of being photographed naked. But I think we can safely assume that many more women appear in *Playboy* for the simple reason that they are paid to. Which is fine. But "because I was paid to" is not the same thing as "I'm taking control of my sexuality."

To hear Hefner tell it, you would think *Playboy* was a veritable cornucopia of different models of sex appeal—*handicapped! aging! buff!* But they gave me a big stack of magazines to flip through and the only variety I saw was the kind of variety you get when you look at a wall of Barbie dolls. Some have darker hair (but most are blonde), some have an ethnic- or professional-themed costume, but they all look very distinctly poured from the same mold. Individuality is erased: It is not part of the formula. When *Playboy*'s Olympian pictorial was out, for example, if you logged on to Playboy.com you were presented with several boxes to click on for previews; the choices were "athletes," "blondes," and "brunettes." It reminded me very much of shopping online for pants: "tweeds," "stretch," "jeans."

Why can't we be sexy and frisky and in control without being commodified? Why do you have to be in *Playboy* to express "I don't think athleticism in women is at odds with being sexy?" If you really believed you were both sexy and athletic, wouldn't it be enough to play your sport with your flawless body and your face gripped with passion in front of the eyes of the world? Rather than showing that we're finally ready to think of "sexy" and "athletic" as mutually inclusive, the Olympian spread revealed how we still imagine these two traits need to be cobbled together: The athletes had to be taken out of context, the purposeful eyes-on-the-prize stare you see on the field had to be replaced with coquettish lash-batting, the fast-moving legs had to be splayed apart.

That women are now doing this to ourselves isn't some kind of triumph, it's depressing. Sexuality is inherent, it is a fundamental part of being human, and it is a lot more complicated than we seem to be willing to admit. Different things are attractive to different people and sexual tastes run wide and wild. Yet somehow, we have accepted as fact the myth that sexiness needs to be something divorced from the everyday experience of being ourselves.

Why have we bought into this? Since when? And how did this happen?

Raunch culture feels perhaps the most alien to aging hippies like my parents—they are all for free love, but none of this looks loving to them; it looks scary, louche, incomprehensible. And, in a way, the emergence of a woman-backed trash culture *is* a rebellion against their values of feminism, egalitarianism, and antimaterialism. But even though this new world of beer and babes feels foreign to sixties revolutionaries, it is actually also a repercussion of the very forces they put in motion—they are the ones who started this.

Two

THE FUTURE THAT
NEVER HAPPENED

Susan Brownmiller was never big on
making concessions. In 1976, shortly after she appeared on the cover of *Time* magazine as a woman of
the year, an interviewer asked her about marriage.
Brownmiller, one of the earliest, most articulate, and
most involved members of the women's liberation
movement, replied, "I would like to be in close association with a man whose work I respect," but said that
it had not happened. "I am not willing to compromise," she explained. "Other women are—their needs
may be greater."

She did not mean "compromise" in the contemporary sense of settling for a man with too little money or too much hair on his back. The struggle for women's equality was the core of her life, and at that time feminists viewed marriage as an arrangement that usually corralled women back toward the subservient lives their mothers had lived, instead of forward into the glorious futures they imagined for their daughters. "It is a horrible truth," Brownmiller told her interviewer, "but the one thing we know now, that men didn't want us to know twenty, thirty, forty years ago is that it is not our fault. It is their fault."

Brownmiller was a fine-featured brunette who had dropped out of Cornell and come to Manhattan to be an actress. She appeared in two off-Broadway performances, but ultimately the stage wasn't for her—she didn't want to play roles, she wanted to speak for herself. Activism within the women's movement proved to be a far better outlet for her self-described "theatrical bravura" and "sense of radical drama." A Brooklyn girl by origin, Brownmiller had always been a high achiever. "Being good at what was expected of me was one of my earliest projects," she wrote in her 1984 best-seller, *Femininity*. "Excellence gave pride and stability to my childhood existence." After she passed through "a stormy adolescence to a stormy maturity," Brownmiller settled into an apartment in Greenwich Village and a career in journalism.

Brownmiller's unshakable clarity of conviction drove her professional life as well as her romantic life.

In the women's movement, the two were inextricably linked—the personal was political. In a famous article called "Sisterhood Is Powerful: A member of the Women's Liberation Movement explains what it's all about," which ran in the *New York Times Magazine* in 1970, Brownmiller wrote, "Women as a class have never subjugated another group; we have never marched off to wars of conquest in the name of the fatherland . . . those are the games men play. *We* see it differently. We want to be neither oppressor nor oppressed. The women's revolution is the final revolution of them all." Brownmiller wasn't interested in tweaking the system already in place. "The goals of liberation go beyond a simple concept of equality," she wrote. What Brownmiller and her radical sisters really wanted was a total transfiguration of society—politics, business, child-rearing, sex, romance, housework, entertainment, academics. And they really believed they would make that happen.

Though she would later admit, "I was not there at the beginning," in the very first sentence of *In Our Time: Memoir of a Revolution,* Brownmiller actually got involved in women's liberation quite early in the movement's development. In September 1968, she attended her first meeting of the group that would become New York Radical Women. Like most of the other attendees, Brownmiller had an activist history; she had already spent two summers in Mississippi volunteering with the civil rights movement. But in the civil rights movement—as in the peace movement, as in the Students for a Democratic Society, as in the New Left in general—women played a supporting role. "Background, education, ideology and experience all primed the New Left women for equality. Yet their experience in the national movement was confusing, grating," writes social historian Todd Gitlin in *The Sixties: Years of Hope, Days of Rage.* "Men sought them out, recruited them, took them seriously, honored their intelligence—then subtly demoted them to girlfriends, wives, note-takers, coffeemakers." It didn't help when Black Power activist Stokely Carmichael made his notorious comment to the Student Nonviolent Coordinating Committee: "The position of women in SNCC is prone."

So women began to meet without men—as a sisterhood—for "consciousness-raising." It was a technique they borrowed from Mao Tse-tung and the "speak bitterness" groups used to energize peasants during the Chinese revolution, which every good radical was reading about in William Hinton's *Fanshen,* an account of rural villagers in Shanxi province absorbing the liberating message of communism and casting off the shackles of bourgeois hierarchy. Interest in feminism had already been invigorated in 1963, when Betty Friedan published *The Feminine Mystique* and subsequently founded the National Organization for Women (NOW). But the women attracted to consciousness-raising were a new breed. "Friedan, the mother of the movement, and the organization that recruited in her image were considered hopelessly bourgeois," Brownmiller wrote. "NOW's emphasis on legislative change left the radicals cold." Friedan and her disciples had fought for succinct advancements, like the desegregation of the *New York Times* help-wanted ads, which were once arranged by gender to distinguish "women's work" from real careers. But Brownmiller, characteristically, was seeking something more momentous and unwieldy: nothing less than the overthrow of the patriarchy, which had to start in the minds and bedrooms of Americans as well as the workplace—change from the inside out.

Brownmiller remembers the evening of January 22, 1973, after the Supreme Court handed down their ruling on *Roe v. Wade* and legalized abortion in this country, as the moment at which she felt the most optimistic about the movement's success. "The momentum was extraordinary, and it culminated with that case," she says, three decades later. "We had the feeling that every woman was listening to us. It was a wonderful feeling—that you had captured the attention of the nation. The Supreme Court could have said, *You're just these fringe women in combat boots.* But they didn't."

After the ruling was announced, the vanguard of the women's movement in New York City headed to the feminist restaurant Mother Courage on West Eleventh Street to celebrate their greatest victory to date. It was the same month Richard Nixon pulled the last U.S. troops out of Vietnam. It was only a few blocks away from the town house blown to bits by the Weathermen, a radical antiwar group that formed out of the ashes of what had been the country's largest grassroots protest organization, Students for a Democratic Society. The Weathermen had accidentally exploded their own town house while developing bombs they intended to detonate at Fort Dix and other Establishment targets such as the U.S. Capitol building, which they successfully hit in the winter of 1971. Years later, former Weatherman Bill Ayers told documentarians Sam Green and Bill Siegel, "I was committed to being a part of what I thought was going to be a really serious and ongoing rebellion; upheaval that had the potential of not just ending the war, but of really overthrowing the Capitalist system and put [ting] in its place something much more humane." Revolution was in the air and triumph seemed imminent.

Mother Courage was a former hole-in-the-wall luncheonette that partners Jill Ward and Dolores Alexander had gutted, decorated with feminist art, and furnished with plain wooden tables. The food, by all accounts, was edible. "We served a mix of Italian, French, American," Alexander says. "I used to joke that it was Continental." Mother Courage was a mediocre restaurant, but it was a cultural sensation. At that time, they were famous, with an international reputation as the place where feminists came to congregate. "We started the restaurant because it was a way to live feminism and be able to afford it," says Alexander, who had also been the first executive director of NOW. "It was an overwhelming success. Everybody from all over the world came in. We had Kate Millet and Gloria Steinem and Susan Sontag . . . Friedan never came in, thank God, because we were feuding. But we had everyone. Everyone who was anyone."

That night at Mother Courage, Susan Brownmiller had the veal, drank a lot of wine, and talked to *everyone.* "Those were glorious times," she says. "We didn't know abortion would be threatened for the next thirty years."

"It was more than jubilant," says Ward. "People just started streaming in. They wanted to rejoice with other women and the place was packed. It was electrifying, it gives me shivers even thinking about it." It was a moment of sororal magic; a time when the shared struggle for women's liberation seemed not only worthwhile but destined to succeed. "It was the type of boisterous excitement where you're jumping up and down for joy," Ward says. "Because it had been such a hard, long battle and everyone was involved either directly or tangentially—whether you were involved with NARAL or letter-writing or consciousness-raising groups, whatever it was. I think the abortion victory was the primary, pivotal moment."

In little more than a decade, a great deal happened that would transform the lives of American women forever. The birth control pill was approved by the FDA in 1960. Congress passed the Equal Pay Act in 1963, which made it illegal to pay a man more than a woman for doing the same job. The Civil Rights Act, passed in 1964, banned discrimination on the basis of race, sex, and religion and, among other things, made it illegal for businesses to reserve specific jobs for men or women or to fire a woman for getting pregnant. The National Organization for Women was founded in 1966, and the National Association for the Repeal of Abortion Laws (NARAL) formed in 1969. (Later, it became the National Abortion Rights Action League, which it remains.) The first edition of *Our Bodies, Ourselves* was published in 1970 and became the quintessential sex guide for feminists and progressives. The landmark anthology *Sisterhood is Powerful*, edited by the feminist poet Robin Morgan, came out that same year. In 1972, the Supreme Court extended the right to birth control to unmarried people with their ruling in *Eisenstadt v. Baird*, and the Equal Rights Amendment passed both houses of Congress. (The ERA, which read "equality of rights under the law shall not be denied or abridged by the United States or any state on account of sex," missed ratification by only three states ten years later.) Finally, in 1973, there was *Roe*.

Many of these events were counted as victories by two revolutionary movements, both of which had a tremendous impact on the reshaping of American womanhood: women's liberation and the sexual revolution. In significant ways, these movements over-lapped. Many of the same people were involved with both causes, and initially some of their key struggles were shared. But ultimately a schism would form between the two movements. And some of the same issues that drove them apart would likewise prove irreconcilably divisive within the women's movement itself.

One of the fundamental initial goals of the women's liberation movement was to advance women's sexual pleasure and satisfaction. The first public articulation of this agenda came from Anne Koedt, a comrade of Susan Brownmiller's at New York Radical Women, who published an essay called "The Myth of Vaginal Orgasm" in a mimeographed pamphlet of their writings that the group put out in 1968. They called it *Notes from the First Year* and sold it to women for fifty cents and to men for a dollar. "The vagina is not a highly sensitive area and is not physiologically constructed to achieve orgasm," Koedt wrote. "We must begin to demand that if a certain sexual position or technique now defined as 'standard' is not mutually conducive to orgasm, then it should no longer be defined as standard." At the time, it was a radical and deeply threatening declaration.

It was substantiated eight years later by the feminist social scientist Shere Hite in her best-seller *The Hite Report: A Nationwide Study of Female Sexuality.* Hite distributed 100,000 questionnaires asking women across the country detailed questions about their sexual practices and, in particular, about how they achieved orgasm. Seventy percent of the 3,019 women who responded said they could not have an orgasm from intercourse, which flew in the face of the teachings of Freud and the generally accepted assumption that missionary position intercourse constituted universally satisfying sex. It was a major blow to the male ego, not to mention the male penis. But the larger reimagining of sexual pleasure as a crucial part of life—one worth fighting for and talking about—and the sense that sexual freedom was ultimately *political*, were shared tenets of both the women's movement and the sexual revolution.

Hugh Hefner, who introduced *Playboy* in 1953, was also trying to reimagine gender roles and influence sexual mores. We may have come to think of him as a glorified dirty old man, but back then Hefner had a cause. (Everyone did.) He was fighting "our ferocious antisexuality, our dark antieroticism," as he told *Look* magazine in 1967. In addition to publishing *Playboy*—which Hefner thought was "like waving a flag of freedom, like screaming 'rebellion' under a dictatorship"—he funded court cases to challenge laws that hindered his vision of healthy sexuality.

Roe and the legalization of the birth control pill—both of which were crucial to feminists—were both helped by funding from Hefner. In 1970, the Playboy Foundation hired a consultant named Cyril

Means, a professor of constitutional law at New York University, to file *amicus curiae*, or friend of the court, briefs in two abortion cases: *Doe v. Bolton* in Georgia and *Roe v. Wade* in Texas. Both cases ultimately went before the U.S. Supreme Court and were, for all practical purposes, consolidated when the ruling was handed down in *Roe*.

The Playboy Foundation also gave grant money to NOW's Legal Defense and Education Fund and supported the ERA; Hefner personally hosted a fundraiser for it at the Playboy Mansion. "I was a feminist before there was such a thing as feminism!" Hefner has said. A mutual friend even tried to set him up on a date with Gloria Steinem before she became famous. (It didn't work out.)

Because of his efforts to promote progressive legislative change and because of the freewheeling approach to sex, nudity, and non-monogamy he advanced through his magazine, his clubs, and his life, Hefner is considered by many to be *the* hero of the sexual revolution. Hefner attracted the radical cultural elite to his magazine. Contributors included Lenny Bruce, Jack Kerouac, and Alex Haley, whose *Playboy* interview with Malcolm X paved the way for his book *Autobiography of Malcolm X*. There were, of course, men of the Left who found the Playboy empire less than groovy. Hefner pursued the cartoonist Robert Crumb for the magazine in the late sixties, to no avail. Crumb, who drew the album cover for Janis Joplin's *Cheap Thrills* and created classic cartoons of the era like Mr. Natural and Keep On Truckin', has said he found the Playboy Mansion "rather alienating and dull . . . I thought it was corny. And the girls seemed barely human to me; I couldn't talk to them." But the average American man was dazzled by Hefner's offer of libertine hedonism: Forget your hang-ups and your Puritan guilt and come get everything you've ever wanted.

Beyond creating a successful brand, Hefner had a vision for a new kind of masculinity, a new kind of man, one who no longer needed to be the duck-hunting outdoorsman, the virtuous patriarch of the forties and fifties. Instead, he was reimagined as a suave gent in a V-neck cashmere sweater, mixing drinks, listening to records, and appreciating the "finer things in life," like jazz and beautiful women. He was freed from domesticity. The feminists' conception of the liberated woman shared a common attribute. She no longer had to toil in the kitchen, benevolent for her brood; she was reconceived as her own, independent person. She was freed from domesticity.

But a shared distaste for conventional family arrangements and repressive laws was the extent of Hefner's ideological compatibility with the women's liberation movement. In 1967, the Italian journalist Oriana Fallaci asked Hefner why he'd chosen the rabbit as the symbol for his empire. He replied:

> The rabbit, the bunny, in America has a sexual
> meaning, and I chose it because it's a fresh ani-

mal, shy, vivacious, jumping—sexy. First it
smells you, then it escapes, then it comes back,
and you feel like caressing it, playing with it. A
girl resembles a bunny. Joyful, joking. Consider
the kind of girl that we made popular: the Play-
mate of the Month. She is never sophisticated, a
girl you cannot really have. She is a young,
healthy, simple girl—the girl next door . . . we
are not interested in the mysterious, difficult
woman, the femme fatale, who wears elegant
underwear, with lace, and she is sad, and somehow mentally filthy. The *Playboy* girl has no
lace, no underwear, she is naked, well-washed
with soap and water, and she is happy.

You can understand why statements like these made
feminists want to throw up. They were specifically
fighting to be seen as *real* people, not sudsy bunnies.
They wanted to show the world that women *were*
"difficult" and "sophisticated," not to mention formi-
dable.

Hefner's sexual revolution seemed to apply only
to men. Women who had the same wealth of sexual
experience as Hefner, who enjoyed elegant underwear
as he enjoyed silk pajamas, were "somehow mentally
filthy." And Hefner backed his taste up with rules.
"The Playboy girls have a very high morality," he said.
"After all, if the Bunnies accept a date, they lose their
job. Private detectives find out if they accept a date."
Women were meant to be ornamental entertainment,

not partners in wildness, and their complicity—their obedience—was policed accordingly in the Playboy empire. Hefner said that he wouldn't mind if his daughter, Christie, then fourteen, appeared in *Playboy* one day; "I would consider it a compliment to me and my work." But again, he would want that to be a *show* of sexiness, not an indication of an unbridled sexuality like his own. "I wouldn't like my daughter to have a promiscuous life. I would not like my daughter to be immoral."

A double standard was unapologetically built into his philosophy. In the first issue of *Playboy*, Hefner's introduction read, "If you're somebody's sister, wife or mother-in-law and picked us up by mistake, please pass us along to the man in your life and get back to your *Ladies Home Companion.*" Free love was edifying for a man, immoral for a woman. Though Hefner was a devoted sexual opportunist himself, he expected total fidelity from his "special girls." "I do not look for equality between man and woman," he said. "I like innocent, affectionate, faithful girls." Really, he liked them the way you like a bunny—as something soft to fondle. "Socially, mentally, I enjoy more being with men. When I want to speak, to think, I stay with men."

To this day, Hefner does not understand why feminists had a problem with him. He maintains that he is a great liberator, a brave iconoclast who battled inhibition for the good of humankind. His opponents are the unenlightened and the uptight. In 2002 he told *Esquire*, "Women were the major beneficiary of the sexual revolution . . . that's where feminism should have been all along. Unfortunately, within feminism, there has been a puritan, prohibitionist element that is antisexual."

He's talking about Susan Brownmiller. Even if she was not personally on his mind when he said that, she was one of the foremost representatives of the "element" he was referring to. Hefner and Brownmiller appeared together on the *Dick Cavett Show* in 1970 to debate pornography (among other things), and as the program progressed, Hefner became increasingly baffled as Brownmiller became increasingly irate. The encounter culminated with Brownmiller suggesting that *he* try coming on stage with a bunny tail on his behind and seeing how well he liked it. In 2005, Hefner told documentarians Fenton Bailey and Randy Barbato that he had been "at a loss for words" during this appearance, because the women's libbers had been "our partners in a revolution to really change sexual values." They may have been bedfellows on *Roe*, but their worldviews were miles apart and their definitions of sexual liberation were mutually exclusive.

In the late seventies, a prominent splinter group of activists, including Brownmiller, Gloria Steinem, Shere Hite, Robin Morgan, the poet Adrienne Rich, and the writers Grace Paley and Audre Lorde, turned their attention to fighting pornography. Brownmiller was one of the founders of the New York chapter of a new group called Women Against Pornography, and they rented out a storefront on Forty-second Street to use as their office. The area was a swamp of peep shows, porn shops, and prostitution—ground zero for the objectification of women—and the feminists set up camp right in the middle of it, in hopes of spreading the gospel of women's liberation and cleaning the place up. There were protests and demonstrations, of course, but Women Against Pornography's trademark was offering guided tours of the neighborhood intended to elucidate the degradation of sex workers. They would bring visiting Benedictine nuns to a strip club to observe the patrons and dancers, or they'd take a curious band of housewives inside a porn shop so they could investigate what it was their husbands were looking at in the garage. Women Against Pornography even led high school class trips.

"Pornography is the theory, rape is the practice," was one of their slogans, coined by Robin Morgan. The idea behind the mantra was also a theme in Brownmiller's first book. In 1975, after four years of squeezing research and writing into her schedule of activism and journalism, Brownmiller published *Against Our Will: Men, Women and Rape*. It became a best-seller, a Book-of-the-Month Club selection, and a movement classic. *Against Our Will* was the first truly comprehensive history of rape ever published. In it, Brownmiller argued that rape was not just an isolated crime like robbery or murder, but a systematic process of demoralization. Of course, we now accept as fact that rape is a grim tactic used in war, or by repressive regimes bent on breaking and subjugating their own people. But Brownmiller went much further. As always, she was working from an emphatic, unwavering conviction: Rape was "nothing more or less than a conscious process of intimidation by which *all men* keep *all women* in a state of fear." Rapists were merely the "front-line masculine shock troops" in the war against women, the "terrorist guerrillas in the longest sustained battle the world has ever known." And pornography was the "undiluted essence of anti-female propaganda" that fed them.

Brownmiller wrote, "I wonder if the ACLU's position [on pornography] might change if, come tomorrow morning, the bookstores and movie theaters lining Forty-second Street in New York City were devoted not to the humiliation of women by rape and torture, as they currently are, but to a systematized, commercially successful propaganda machine depicting the sadistic pleasures of gassing Jews or lynching blacks? Is this analogy extreme? Not if you are a woman who is conscious of the ever-present threat of rape."

It wasn't just Hugh Hefner who found this position "antisexual." Within the women's liberation movement, the question of how to represent sex— even the question of how to *have* sex—became divisive. Two distinct and passionately oppositional factions developed. On the one hand there were the antiporn feminists, and on the other, there were the women who felt that if feminism was about freedom for women, then women should be free to look at or appear in pornography. Screaming fights became a regular element of feminist conferences once the "pornography wars" got underway in the late seventies.

The term "sex-positive feminist" first came into use at this time. It was employed by the members of the women's movement who wanted to distinguish themselves from the antiporn faction. But, of course, all of the feminists thought they were being sex-positive. Brownmiller and her compatriots felt they were liberating women from degrading sexual stereotypes and a culture of male domination and—consequently—making room for greater female sexual pleasure. Her opponents thought they were fighting a new brand of in-house repression. "Sometimes [there] were emotional defenses of free speech, but to our bewilderment, we also saw that some women identified their sexuality with the S/M pictures we found degrading," Brownmiller wrote. "They claimed we were condemning their minds and behavior, and I guess we were." Everyone was fighting for freedom, but when it came to sex, freedom meant different things to different people.

Rifts deepened in 1983, when Catharine MacKinnon, a radical feminist legal scholar at the University of Minnesota, and Andrea Dworkin, a visiting professor with a fondness for overalls who had authored the controversial books *Woman Hating* (1974) and *Pornography: Men Possessing Women* (1981), drafted a city ordinance positioning porn as a civil rights violation against women. Their ordinance was twice vetoed by the mayor of Minneapolis, but Dworkin and MacKinnon were subsequently summoned by the conservative city council of Indianapolis, Indiana, which was eager to rid their city of smut and wanted the antiporn feminists' help. The city council and the Republican mayor of Indianapolis, William Hudnut, were opposed to core feminist goals like abortion rights and the ERA, but Dworkin and MacKinnon felt so outraged by what they viewed as pornography's assault on female dignity that they joined forces with the conservatives anyway.

Dworkin was a former prostitute who had been beaten by her husband and sexually assaulted by doctors when she was taken to the Women's House of Detention in New York City in 1965 after participating in a march against the Vietnam War. In 1995, she told the British writer Michael Moorcock, "I looked at pornography to try to understand what had happened to me. And I found a lot of information, about power and the mechanisms by which the subordination of women is sexualised." The ordinance she'd crafted with MacKinnon was signed into Indianapolis law in 1984. Soon thereafter, the law was deemed unconstitutional and overturned by federal courts. But many feminists never forgave Dworkin and MacKinnon—and, by association, all antiporn feminists—for getting into bed with the right wing. To them, it symbolized exactly the kind of termagant moralism and prudery they felt were corrupting their movement.

"Suddenly, pornography became the enemy . . . sex in general became the enemy!" says Candida Royalle, a sex-positive feminist then, a director of adult films geared to female viewers now. "The women's movement, in a way, was starting to be co-opted. I think the MacKinnonites and the Dworkinites definitely moved in at that point. And remember, Dworkin is the one who said intercourse is an act of rape, *inherently* an act of rape."

Royalle is not alone in interpreting Dworkin's work this way; both *Playboy* and *Time* magazine have cited this idea as hers. Dworkin for her part has said this is not a message she intended to convey. In the preface to the tenth anniversary addition of her book *Intercourse*, she wrote about why an imaginary (male) reader might mistakenly think she was saying all intercourse is rape:

> [I]f one's sexual experience has always and without exception been based on dominance—not only overt acts but also metaphysical and ontological assumptions—how can one read this book? The end of male dominance would mean—in the understanding of such a man— the end of sex. If one has eroticized a differential in power that allows for force as a natural and inevitable part of intercourse, how could one understand that this book does not say that

all men are rapists or that all intercourse is rape? Equality in the realm of sex is an antisexual idea if sex requires domination in order to register as sensation. As sad as I am to say it, the limits of the old Adam—and the material power he still has, especially in publishing and media—have set limits on the public discourse (by both men and women) about this book.

I don't think Dworkin is being quite fair here. The bias against her work also has something to do with people being put off by her extremist proclamations. Consider this snippet from an article she wrote called "Dear Bill and Hillary" for *The Guardian* (London) in 1998:

Bill Clinton's fixation on oral sex—non-reciprocal oral sex—consistently puts women in states of submission to him. It's the most fetishistic, heartless, cold sexual exchange that one could imagine . . . I have a modest proposal. It will probably bring the FBI to my door, but I think that Hillary should shoot Bill and then President Gore should pardon her.

This was more than Candida Royalle had bargained for. She had first gotten involved with the women's movement in her late teens, when she attended consciousness-raising workshops in the Bronx and organized free clinics where local women could come for PAP smears and pelvic exams. For Royalle, it was an ironic disappointment to see the movement go in what felt like an anti-sex direction, because one of the most powerful things she'd gleaned from feminism was a heightened sense of connection with her own body, one area in particular: "A lot of girls don't grow up knowing they have a clitoris," she says. "I remember reading the very first edition of *Our Bodies, Ourselves,* and it was that book that made me understand how I could have an orgasm. I had a boyfriend for years who I'd been sleeping with and I couldn't understand why it was never enough! But then I saw that book and there was this diagram, and it said, you know, you rub this thing long enough and then you have an orgasm. And I thought, *Oh, I think I'll try that.* That was a big part of the movement back then. Sexual liberation was really a lot of what it was about. Sadly, that changed."

Now middle-aged, Royalle is a bright-eyed blonde who wears wacky glasses and lives in a roomy apartment in Greenwich Village decorated with dozens of photos of herself in various phases and ages and hair colors. "I think it was the summer of 1970 that I went with a friend over to Corsica and we rented mopeds and spent a night in the mountains and took a hit of mescaline, and there's all these really fun pictures of us," she says. "There I am pos-ing—probably flying—with my copy of *Sisterhood Is Powerful.* Like it's the Bible." (Keep in mind: *Sister-*

hood Is Powerful, the anthology of feminist writings, was edited by Robin Morgan, the same woman who postulated "pornography is the theory, rape is the practice.") "It was this fun moment, very much about sisterhood," says Royalle, "but things changed. It became sort of the opposite. It started about two-thirds of the way in . . . you could feel the subtle shift. I remember feeling that I was becoming a minority; that I was not sticking to the party line because I did have a boyfriend, and it was kind of like I was sleeping with the enemy. There was a real move to rejecting heterosexual relationships and embracing lesbianism, or embracing separatism. There are women who won't want to hear this, but I think a lot of women were calling themselves lesbians who, in the end, really weren't. Because it was the thing to do, it was more politically acceptable."

In this environment, Royalle felt almost as restricted as she had back in the fifties, only now she was rebelling against feminist sisters instead of an overprotective patriarchy. She left New York for San Francisco to pursue a career as an artist. Royalle paid the bills by modeling for other artists, which led to an offer to appear in an art film, which led to a career in pornography. "During that time I was living amongst a group of people who were fiercely independent, these outrageous drag queens. We had sex with whoever we wanted. We did drugs whenever we wanted. No one could tell us what to do. So when I needed extra money and the opportunity to be in a movie came up, it wasn't like *Ooh, is this acceptable?* It wasn't a big deal . . . there was no AIDS yet and it was still a time of sexual adventurousness."

Royalle knew her movement sisters wouldn't see it that way. "I pretty much lost touch with them. I knew that what I was doing would be seen as a betrayal, that I was taking part in something that was considered degrading to women. It was my way of going to the other extreme," she says. "Rebelling against the too-radical uptightness that was turning a movement I loved into these old biddies telling me we shouldn't have relationships with men."

Imagine how Susan Brownmiller must have felt. Her vision had always been crystalline, her beliefs ardent. She had become engaged in the women's liberation movement when it was a unified, sure-footed quest for change, and suddenly she was in a maze of contradictions. Now there were "feminists" working with conservative Republicans. There were "feminist" pornographers. There were separatist "feminists," and there was a highly vocal contingent of S/M lesbian "feminists." What had been clear and beautiful was now messy and contentious.

"There had been an innocent bravery to the anti-pornography campaign in the beginning, a quixotic tilting at windmills in the best radical feminist tradition," Brownmiller writes in *In Our Time*. But it degenerated into a deadlock. "Movement women were waging a battle over who owned feminism, or who held the trademark to speak in its name, and plainly on this issue no trademark existed." Sisterhood had been powerful, but infighting and scoldings grew exhausting. Movement women were becoming depleted. "Ironically, the anti-porn initiative constituted the last gasp of radical feminism," writes Brownmiller. "No issue of comparable passion has arisen to take its place."

On the Web site for the group CAKE, it says "The new sexual revolution is where sexual equality and feminism finally meet." CAKE throws monthly parties in New York City and London at which women can "explore female sexuality" and experience "feminism in action." They lament, "Back in the day, because fighting sexual abuse was the priority, mainstream feminism tended to treat sexuality like a dark horse." CAKE wants to fix all that. Founders Emily Kramer and Melinda Gallagher cite Hugh Hefner as a hero.

CAKE parties are so prominent they were featured on an episode of *Law & Order* in 2004—renamed Tart parties, which actually seems like a more apt moniker when you think about it. (In an interview with ABC's *20/20*, Kramer and Gallagher said that they chose "cake" as their name because it is a slang term for female genitalia, and connotes something "gooey, sweet, yummy, sexy, sticky.") They have 35,000 online subscribers, a book deal, a Web boutique through which they sell tank tops and vibrators, and a Showtime reality pilot in the works.

CAKE is also a sort of hypersexual sorority. You have to pledge to get in, which involves writing an essay and paying a hundred dollars. Then, if you are accepted, you get regular e-mails from CAKE's founders called "CAKE Bytes," with commentary on everything from the Bush Administration's war of attrition on abortion rights to the perceived weaknesses of *Sex and the City*. Kramer and Gallagher engage in a certain amount of old-school grassroots organizing— they arranged for a bus to take women from Manhattan to Washington, D.C., for the April 25, 2004, March for Women's Lives, for example—but their parties are what have put them on the map.

Themes have ranged from "Striptease-a-thons" to porn parties, and the events are thrown at upscale venues like the W hotels and velvet-rope clubs throughout Manhattan and London. CAKE made the front page of the *New York Post* with one of their early parties in 2001, at which two guests, the adult film actors Marie Silva and Jack Bravo, had intercourse and oral sex inside CAKE's designated "Freak Box," a steel closet with a camera inside offering everyone outside live streaming video of the shagging-in-action projected onto huge screens throughout the party.

In the fall of 2003, they threw an event called "CAKE Underground" at a club called B'lo in Manhattan. On the e-vite, they said it was an opportunity to "witness the REAL LIFE ACTUALIZATION of women's sexual desires."

They had hired a dwarf to work the elevator. The words "exhibitionism" and "voyeurism" and the letters XXX were projected onto the club walls. *The hos they wanna fuck,* 50 Cent boomed over the sound system. I was presented with a sticker of a woman's hip to knee region clad in garters and fishnets above the words, "ASK ME: If I know where my G-spot is." (I am strangely shy about discussing the topography of my vagina with strangers, so I declined to wear the sticker as instructed by the woman in pigtails at the door.)

Gallagher, a stunning thirty-year-old with long chestnut hair and the physique of a short model, and Kramer, who wore punky clothes and a wary expression as she surveyed her party, have adopted the women's movement's early policy on admissions to anti-rape speak-outs: Men pay double and have to be accompanied by a woman. That did not seem to hurt the male attendance at B'lo. The room was packed with women wearing extremely revealing clothing or just lingerie, and young men in jeans and button-down shirts who couldn't believe their luck.

A blonde in a white fur jacket over a pink lace bra sucked a lollipop while she waited for her $11 vodka tonic at the bar. A fellow in his early thirties wearing a suit with no tie asked her, "Have you ever had a threesome?"

"What?" she said. Then she realized that he was only reading off the ASK ME sticker she had plastered on her right breast. "Sorry," she said. "Yeah, I've had like four."

At around eleven, a troop of CAKE dancers got on the stage in the center of the huge room. They wore thigh-high patent leather boots, fishnets, and satin bra and panty sets the colors of cotton candy and clear skies.

At first, they shimmied onstage like garden variety lusty club-goers. But then a visiting crew from Showtime turned on their cameras and when the lights hit the dancers they started humping each other as if possessed. A blonde woman with improbably large breasts immediately bent over and a dancer with a souped-up Mohawk got behind her and started grinding her crotch against the other woman's rear end.

Many, many men formed a pack around the stage and most pumped their fists in the air to the beat of the music and the humping.

"The girls are much hotter here than at the last party," a mousy young woman in a gray skirt-suit told her friend, who was in similar straight-from-work attire.

"You think? Look at that one," she said, pointing at Mohawk. "She's basically flat!"

A twenty-five-year-old assistant with lovely green eyes and an upswept ponytail was looking back and forth between the dancers onstage and her ex-boyfriend, who was having a smile-filled conversation with a sleek woman in a black bra. "What should I do?" she said. "Should I go over there? Should I go home?"

The next day, I called her at her office at around

one o'clock. (She was so hung over I could almost smell the alcohol through the phone.) "He went home with that girl," she said. "I ended up staying really late. My friend and I were in the back room and we got really drunk and kind of hooked up with like seven people. Mostly girls. The guys just watched. Uck."

Many of the conflicts between the women's liberation movement and the sexual revolution and within the women's movement itself were left unresolved thirty years ago. What we are seeing today is the residue of that confusion. CAKE is an example of the strange way people are ignoring the contradictions of the past, pretending they never existed, and putting various, conflicting ideologies together to form one incoherent brand of raunch feminism.

Some of this is motivated by a kind of generational rebellion. Embracing raunch so casually is a way for young women to thumb our noses at the intense fervor of second-wave feminists (which both Kramer and Gallagher's mothers were). Nobody wants to turn into their mother. Certainly, this generation can afford to be less militant than Susan Brownmiller's compatriots because the world is now a different place. In their book *Manifesta: Young Women, Feminism, and the Future* (2000), Jennifer Baumgardner and Gloria Steinem's former assistant Amy Richards tell us they are different from their "serious sisters of the sixties and seventies" because they live in a time when the "feminist movement has such a firm and organic toehold in women's lives."

But raunch feminism is not *only* a rebellion. It is also a garbled attempt at continuing the work of the women's movement. "Whether it's volunteering at a women's shelter, attending an all women's college or a speak-out for Take Back the Night, or dancing at a strip club," write Baumgardner and Richards, "whenever women are gathered together there is great potential for individual women, and even the location itself, to become radicalized." They don't explain what "radicalized" means to them, so we are left to wonder if it is their way of saying "enlightened" or "sexually charged" or if to them those are the same things. In this new formulation of raunch feminism, stripping is as valuable to elevating womankind as gaining an education or supporting rape victims. Throwing a party where women grind against each other in their underwear while fully-clothed men watch them is suddenly part of the same project as marching on Washington for reproductive rights. According to Baumgardner and Richards, "watching TV shows *(Xena! Buffy!)* can . . . contain feminism in action"—just as CAKE bills their parties as "feminism in action." Based on these examples, it would seem raunch feminism in action is pretty easy to achieve: The basic requirements are hot girls and small garments.

I had occasion to talk to Erica Jong, one of the

most famous sex-positive feminists—"one of the most interviewed people in the world," as she's put it—on the thirtieth anniversary of her novel *Fear of Flying.* "I was standing in the shower the other day, picking up my shampoo," she said. "It's called 'Dumb Blonde.' I thought, *Thirty years ago you could not have sold this.* I think we have lost consciousness of the way our culture demeans women." She was quick to tell me that she "wouldn't pass a law against the product or call the PC police." But, she said, "let's not kid ourselves that this is liberation. The women who buy the idea that flaunting your breasts in sequins is power—I mean, I'm for all that stuff—but let's not get so into the tits and ass that we don't notice how far we haven't come. Let's not confuse that with real power. I don't like to see women fooled."

Nouvelle raunch feminists are not concocting this illogic all by themselves. Some of it they learned in school. A fervid interest in raunchy representations of sex and a particular brand of women's studies are both faddish in academia now, and the two are frequently presented side by side, as if they formed a seamless, comprehensible totality. I went to Wesleyan University at the height of the "politically correct" craze in the nineties. Wesleyan was the kind of school that had coed showers, on principle. There were no "fresh*men*," only "frosh." There were no required courses, but there was a required role-play as part of frosh orientation in which we had to stand up and say "I'm a homosexual" and "I'm an Asian-American," so that we would understand what it felt like to be part of an oppressed group. It didn't make a lot of sense, but such was the way of PC.

I remember a meeting we once had, as members of the English majors committee, with the department faculty: We were there to tell them about a survey we'd given out to English majors, the majority of whom said they wanted at least one classics course to be offered at our college. We all bought the party line that such a class should never be *required* because that would suggest that Dead White Men were more important than female and nonwhite writers. But we figured it couldn't do any harm for them to *offer* one canonical literature course for those of us who wanted to grasp the references in the contemporary Latin American poetry we were reading in every other class. It seemed like a pretty reasonable request to me. After I made my pitch for it, the woman who was head of the department at that time looked at me icily and said, "I would never *teach* at a school that offered a course like that."

It was a pretty weird time. It was not okay to have a class tracing the roots of Western literature, but it was okay to offer a class on porn, as a humanities professor named Hope Weissman did, in which students engaged in textual analysis of money shots and three-ways. In an environment in which everyone was talking about "constructions" of gender and pulling apart their culturally conditioned assumptions about everything, it seemed natural to take apart our culturally conditioned assumptions about sex—i.e., that it should be the manifestation of affection, or even attraction. And sex wasn't just something we read about in class, it was the most popular sport on campus. (This became clear to me almost immediately: When I first visited Wesleyan as a seventeen-year-old senior in high school, I was taken to the cafeteria, some classes, and a Naked Party. I remember giant crepe paper penis and vagina decorations.) Group sex, to say nothing of casual sex, was de rigueur. By the time I was in college we heard considerably less than people had in the eighties about "No means no," possibly because we always said yes.

The modish line of academic thinking was to do away with "works" of literature or art and focus instead on "texts," which were always products of the social conditions in which they were produced. We were trained to look at the supposedly all-powerful troika of race, class, and gender and how they were dealt with in narrative—and that narrative could be anywhere, in *Madame Bovary* or *Debbie Does Dallas*—rather than to analyze artistic quality, which we were told was really just code for the ideals of the dominant class.

Kramer is also a product of this academic moment. When I met her, she was not long out of Columbia University, where she majored in gender studies and wrote her thesis on "how the power dynamics of sexuality should ideally allow for both men and women to explore, express and define sexuality for themselves." In an e-mail, she told me she started CAKE with Gallagher because she felt the "mainstream messaging related to sexuality either pitted female sexuality *in terms of* male sexuality—like articles in popular women's magazines on how to please your man—or defined sexuality as dominated by men . . . like critical feminist texts." (Kramer's writing here has echoes of Shere Hite, who wrote in the preface to the original *Hite Report*, published in 1976, "female sexuality has been seen essentially as a response to male sexuality and intercourse. There has rarely been any acknowledgment that female sexuality might have a complex nature of its own which would be more than just the logical counterpart of {what we think of as} male sexuality.") Kramer was edging in on a solution. "I thought there should be another option for women, and began to formulate a theory behind what that option should be." She wouldn't spell her theory out for me, but presumably CAKE parties are its embodiment.

Despite Kramer and Gallagher's magniloquence on "mainstream messaging" and "feminism in action," I was reminded of CAKE parties a few months later when I attended an event in a giant parking lot in Los Angeles for *Maxim* magazine's "Hot 100," their annual assessment of the hundred hottest famous women. People were lined up in scantily clad droves on Vine Street, waiting to get rejected when their names were mysteriously found missing from the phone book–sized list at the door. Past the gatekeepers, there was an orange jeep and two hired girls in bikini tops and black cowboy boots who spent the evening smiling, arching their backs, and buffing the vehicle with bandannas.

This was a high-profile party with press coverage and celebrities (Denzel Washington, Christian Slater, the model Amber Valletta, the singer Macy Gray, and of course, Paris Hilton). Somehow, a pair of inordinately geeky-looking guys who were actually wearing backpacks got in. One turned to the other and said, "See that black girl in front of you? Look at her face. She's so fine." The dance floor was a sea of naked legs perched on high-heeled sandals.

The party extended into an adjacent warehouse, where a smoke machine kept the air gauzy, and in the center, there was a large bed on a raised dais on which two girls, one Asian, one blonde, both in lingerie and pigtails, had an extended pillow fight. Behind the bar, tall females in white feathered tops danced on poles, their faces set in masks of lascivious contempt. Keith Blanchard, then *Maxim*'s editor-in-chief, told me, "It's a sexy night!"

To me, "sexy" is based on the inexplicable overlap of character and chemicals that happens between people . . . the odd sense that you have something primal in common with another person whom you may love, or you may barely even like, that can only be expressed through the physical and psychological exchange that is sex. When I'm in the plastic "erotic" world of high, hard tits and long nails and incessant pole dancing—whether I'm at a CAKE party, walking past a billboard of Jenna Jameson in Times Square, or dodging pillows at the Maxim Hot 100—I don't feel titillated or liberated or aroused. I feel bored, and kind of tense.

In defense of CAKE parties, Gallagher told a reporter from *Elle* magazine, "*you* try getting 800 people to behave in a feminist way!" To be sure, that's no small project. But we have to wonder how displaying hot chicks onstage in exactly the same kind of miniature outfits they've always been in moves things in the right direction. If CAKE is promoting *female* sexual culture, I can't believe there aren't other ways to excite women. I even believe there are other ways to excite men.

Kramer said, "CAKE's mission is to change public perceptions about female sexuality," and their Web site claims they seek to "redefine the current boundaries [of] female sexuality." If the whole point is change and redefinition, then I wonder why the CAKE imagery—from the porn movies they project on the walls at their parties to the insignia they use on their Web site, a sexy cartoon silhouette of a lean, curvy lady with wind-swept hair and her hand on her hip—looks so utterly of a piece with every other bimbo pictorial I've seen in my life. Why is this the "new feminism" and not what it looks like: the old objectification?

Despite what can fairly be called a campaign of begging on my part, Kramer and Gallagher refused to answer questions about why they can't achieve their "female-directed sexual revolution" without the constant presence of taut, waxed strippers. They were evasive, I think, on the subject of girls on display because they can't quite figure out what else to do. And it *is* a tough one—how do you publicly express the concept "sexy" without falling back on the old hot-chicks-in-panties formula? It's a challenge that requires imagination and creativity that they do not possess. They haven't yet found a way to enact the redefinition they are advocating, so they are wishing for feminist justification where none exists. The truth is that the new conception of raunch culture as a path to liberation rather than oppression is a convenient (and lucrative) fantasy with nothing to back it up.

Or, as Susan Brownmiller put it when I asked her what she made of all this, "You think you're being brave, you think you're being sexy, you think you're *transcending* feminism. But that's bullshit."

On August 26, 1970, tens of thousands of women went on "strike" from their homes and families and jobs to march down Fifth Avenue on the fiftieth anniversary of women's suffrage. The action was Betty Friedan's brainchild, and she'd announced the idea of a "Women's Strike for Equality" in an infamous two-hour speech at NOW's fourth national conference—just minutes after she was voted off the board of the organization she'd started back in 1966.

"They kicked Betty upstairs; everybody had had it with her at that point," remembers Jacqui Ceballos, a former president of New York NOW and, at various other times in her seventy-eight years, a student of astrology, a television actress, and the founder of the first opera house in Bogotá, Colombia. "She had created some really very bad vibes with her position on lesbians and she had alienated everybody." (Friedan notoriously called lesbian feminists a "lavender menace.") "Oh, if I can tell you how they humiliated Betty Friedan! One time they sent her down to get coffee. Yes, ma'am! So she's going to have this big strike and march. And I'm telling you, she had no one to work with. No one! But I went to Betty and I said, 'I'll help you.' I got the Socialist Worker's Party in on it and everyone was nervous about those women, but let me tell you: They were organizers!"

In an inspired publicity stunt, Ceballos and her comrades took over the Statue of Liberty. "Put a sign on her saying WOMEN OF THE WORLD UNITE! MARCH ON AUGUST 26! I always get excited thinking about it because it was really something. We'd already had women go and case the statue and they knew *everything:* They knew what the weather was going to be like and they knew the wind angle and they knew how to hang up these two huge banners. So we got 'em up and then the guards were banging around at the entrance of the statue, but the mayor John Lindsay called and said, *Let the women be!* Oh, it was a huge event."

The committee organizing the march also held a traditional press conference to enlist supporters. "We invited the whole press and Bella Abzug and we invited Gloria Steinem because she had been making feminist remarks, and then Betty didn't show! She was stuck in traffic," Ceballos says. "The press was getting antsy and I realized we were going to lose them if something didn't happen, so I jumped up and started saying things that were in my head—saying we were going to do all these things that I had no idea if we were going to do. I told everyone that fifty thousand women would march and then I had to get 'em. There must have been no news that summer, because, I'm telling you, it went around the world. It was scary as hell! I remember running around Manhattan with Jill Ward," *Mother Courage*'s cofounder, "putting flyers about the coming march everywhere we could find a place. At one point we were driving up Park Avenue at rush hour, stopped at a red light, and in the car next to us the couple was obviously arguing, and the woman was crying. Jill jumped out of her driver's seat, tapped on the window, and gave the woman a flyer.

"All day long before the march at five o'clock we had actions," Ceballos continues. "We went to restaurants that were for men only; we did a prayer service. They say we had no sense of humor, but it was hilarious: We put out the *NOW York Times* and had a wedding announcement with a picture of the groom, and we gave out awards to the Biggest Male Chauvinist and all that kind of thing. Everyone in town was waiting for us. By the time the march came, after doing actions all day, I turned the corner onto Fifth Avenue and there were *thousands* of women. I couldn't see the end of the line. It was not a march like the early suffragists. We were dancing and singing and running and there were thousands of people watching us. After our march, Kate Millett said, 'We are a movement now.' And that's how I felt: We are no longer a group of crazy radicals, we're a political movement. At that point, even my mother got involved."

In the days when feminism was fun, women's liberation was an adventure that involved stakeouts and bloodless coups and victory celebrations for the conquering heroines. The women's movement introduced revolutionary ideas that caught on so thoroughly they now seem self-evident. That women don't automatically have to be mothers or (even) wives. That women are entitled to their constitutional guarantee of equal protection under the law. That women ought to be eligible to attend top schools (Princeton and Yale did not begin admitting female students until 1969; Harvard shared some classes with the women of Radcliffe as early as 1943 but did not fully integrate until 1972; Columbia was all male for undergraduates until 1983). That women should not be discriminated against in the workplace. That there is such a thing as a clitoris.

In the late sixties and seventies, even women

who had no direct contact with the movement felt the ripple effects of feminist activism in one way or another. The ordinary women who weren't celebrating *Roe* at Mother Courage or storming the Statue of Liberty were still seeing these events on television and reading about them in the paper. Women's lib was a media sensation and a far-reaching grassroots effort. At the height of the movement there were women's consciousness-raising groups in every major city in this country, spreading the message to the masses.

Ultimately, in addition to the obvious freedoms feminism brought to non-movement women, it also affected their vocabularies and their wardrobes— their taste as well as their consciousness. As Brownmiller writes in *In Our Time*, "even the 'Women's Lib look'—the brazen disregard for makeup and bras and a preference for jeans and long, unkempt hair that affronted Middle America—was taken up by fashion trendies as a sexy statement." In addition to being crucial and revolutionary, feminism was cool.

In recent years, the term "feminism" has fallen further and further out of favor. According to a 2001 Gallup poll, only 25 percent of women considered themselves feminists, down a percentage point from the 1999 survey. Some of the concepts and the lexicon introduced by the women's movement remain modish, however: We are still encouraged by fashion and media and Hollywood and each other to be "strong women." "Liberation" and "empowerment" are still buzzwords, but they once referred to bucking the system, going on strike against submission, adopting a brazen, braless, unshaven, untrammeled approach to life. These terms have since been drained of meaning. Instead of hairy legs, we have waxed vaginas; the free-flying natural woman boobs of yore have been hoisted with push-up bras or "enhanced" into taut plastic orbs that stand perpetually at attention. What has moved into feminism's place as the most pervasive phenomenon in American womanhood is an almost opposite style, attitude, and set of principles.

Ceballos, who now runs a group called the Veteran Feminists of America out of her hometown, Lafayette, Louisiana, was also present in 1968 in Atlantic City when feminists protested the Miss America Pageant and the urban myth of bra-burners was born. "It was against the law to burn bras or anything else, but there was a 'freedom trash can' out on the boardwalk and we threw in anything we thought was oppressive to women," she says. The basic protest went like so: "Women in our society are forced daily to compete for male approval, enslaved by ludicrous beauty standards that we ourselves are conditioned to take seriously and to accept!"

"At that time, Miss America had to stand up and say her aspiration was to be a good wife and mother and then they would send her over to Vietnam. To excite the boys! Oh, it was just disgusting," says Ceballos. "Some of the women broke into the actual pageant and they were arrested with the great Flo

Kennedy." (Kennedy, a lawyer, writer, and activist, started the Feminist Party to support black congresswoman Shirley Chisholm's run for the presidency and served as legal defense for Valerie Solanis, the woman who shot Andy Warhol.) "Of course, this is the kind of news that gets around. That's why we chose to do it!"

One of the reporters covering the protest was Lindsy Van Gelder from the *New York Post*, who compared the trashing of bras to the burning of draft cards, and ever since people have mentally connected feminists with an imaginary lingerie inferno. "We weren't allowed to burn bras or anything else," says Ceballos, "but I did throw out my son's *Playboy*. And I said, 'Women! Use your brains, not your bodies!'"

Three

FEMALE
CHAUVINIST PIGS

On the first warm day of spring 2000, the organization New York Women in Film & Television threw a brunch to honor Sheila Nevins, a twenty-six-year veteran of HBO and their president of documentary and family programming. It was held in a grand, street-level room off Park Avenue, in which they'd assembled an impressive selection of stylish women, seasonal berries, and high-end teas. Through the windows you could see the passing streams of yellow taxis sparkling in the midtown sunlight.

But the vibe was more *Lifetime Intimate Portrait* than *Sex and the City*. "I was growing up in a society where women were quiet so I got to listen," Nevins reflected from the podium, where she sat lovely and serene in a pale pink shawl. "I like to laugh, I like to cry, the rest is paperwork."

Nevins is a big deal. She was once profiled as one of the "25 Smartest Women in America" along with Tina Brown, Susan Sontag, and Donna Brazile in *Mirabella*. *Crain's* has called Nevins "a revered player." Under her stewardship, HBO programs and documentary films have won seventy-one Emmy awards, thirteen Oscars, and twenty-two George Foster Peabody awards, including Nevins's own personal Peabody. In 2000, Nevins was inducted into the Broadcasting and Cable Hall of Fame, and she has received Lifetime Achievement Awards from the International Documentary Association and the Banff Television Festival. In 2002, Nevins was named the National Foundation for Jewish Culture's "Woman of Inspiration." She is an elegant blonde with a husband and a son and a glamorous, lucrative career that even involves an intimidating level of gravitas: She has overseen the making of films about the Holocaust, cancer, and war orphans.

At that breezy spring breakfast, all the women wore glazed, reverential expressions as they picked at their melon wedges and admired Nevins's sharp wit, keen intellect, and zebra-printed slides. "Who opened your career doors for you?" one wanted to know.

"Me," Nevins replied.

A tweedy gentleman with a bow tie started his question with, "I'm just the token guy . . ."

Nevins gave a little snort and said, "You're all tokens," and everyone had a good laugh.

But then a curly-haired woman in the back brought up *G-String Divas,* a late-night "docu-soap" Nevins executive produced, which treated audiences to extended showings of T & A sandwiched between interviews with strippers about tricks of the trade and their real-life sexual practices. "Why would a woman—a middle-aged woman with a child—make a show about strippers?" the woman asked. Everyone was stunned.

Nevins whipped around in her chair. "You're talking fifties talk! Get with the program!" she barked. "I love the sex stuff, I love it! What's the big deal?"

In fact, there *was* something vaguely anachronistic about this woman compared to the rest with their blowouts and lip liner. She adjusted her eyeglasses, visibly shaken, but persisted. "Why is it still the case that if we're going to have a series about women on television, it has to be about their bodies and their sexuality?"

Nevins shook her head furiously. "Why is it that women will still go after women taking their clothes off and not after all the injustices in the workplace? I don't get it! As if women taking off their clothes is disgusting and degrading. Not being able to feed your kids, *that's* disgusting and degrading!"

"But . . ."

"Everyone has to bump and grind for what they

want," Nevins interrupted. "Their bodies are their in-
struments and if I had that body I'd play it like a
Stradivarius!"

"But . . ."

"The women are beautiful and the men are
fools! What's the problem?"

"But you're not really answering my question."

Of course not. Because part of the answer is that
nobody wants to be the frump at the back of the
room anymore, the ghost of women past. It's just not
cool. What *is* cool is for women to take a guy's-eye
view of pop culture in general and live, nude girls in
particular. *You're worried about strippers?* Nevins
seemed on the verge of hollering at her inquisitor,
*Honey, they could teach you a thing or two about
where it's at!* Nevins was threatening something she
clearly considered far worse than being objectified:
being out of touch.

If you are too busy or too old or too short to make
a Stradivarius of yourself, then the least you can do is
appreciate that achievement in others, or so we are
told. If you still suffer from the (hopelessly passé) conviction that valuing a woman on the sole basis of her
hotness is, if not disgusting and degrading, then at
least dehumanizing, if you still cling to the (patheti-
cally deluded) hope that a more abundant enjoyment
of the "sex stuff" could come from a reexamination of
old assumptions, then you are clearly stuck in the past
(and you'd better get a clue, but quick).

If I told you that I'd met someone who executive

produces a reality show about strippers, who becomes irritable and dismissive when faced with feminist debate, and who is a ferocious supporter of lap dances, you might reasonably assume I was talking about a man—the kind of man we used to call a Male Chauvinist Pig. But no. I'm talking about the Jewish Woman of Inspiration. I'm talking about an urbane, articulate, extremely successful woman who sits on a high perch in the middle of the mainstream, and I *could* be talking about any number of other women, because the ideas and emotions Nevins gave voice to are by no means uniquely her own: They are the status quo.

We decided long ago that the Male Chauvinist Pig was an unenlightened rube, but the Female Chauvinist Pig (FCP) has risen to a kind of exalted status. She is post-feminist. She is funny. She *gets it*. She doesn't mind cartoonish stereotypes of female sexuality, and she doesn't mind a cartoonishly macho response to them. The FCP asks: Why throw your boyfriend's *Playboy* in a freedom trash can when you could be partying at the Mansion? Why worry about *disgusting* or *degrading* when you could be giving—or getting—a lap dance yourself? Why try to beat them when you can join them?

There's a way in which a certain lewdness, a certain crass, casual manner that has at its core a me-Tarzan-you-Jane mentality can make people feel equal. It makes us feel that way because we are all Tarzan now, or at least we are all pretending to be.

For a woman like Nevins, who "grew up in a society where women were quiet" and still managed to open all her career doors herself, this is nothing new. She has been functioning—with enormous success—in a man's world for decades. Somewhere along the line she had to figure out how to be one of the guys.

Nevins is (still) what used to be known as a "loophole woman," an exception in a male-dominated field whose presence supposedly proves its penetrability. (The phrase was coined by Caroline Bird in her book *Born Female: The High Cost of Keeping Women Down*, published in 1968.) Women in powerful positions in entertainment were a rare breed when Nevins started out, and they remain so today. In 2003, women held only 17 percent of the key roles—executive producers, producers, directors, writers, cinematographers, and editors—in making the top 250 domestic grossing films. (And progress is stalled: The percentage of women working on top films hasn't changed since 1998.) Meanwhile on television, men outnumbered women by approximately four to one in behind-the-scenes roles in the 2002–2003 prime-time season, which was also the case for the preceding four seasons. What the statistics indicate more clearly than the entertainment industry's permeability is a woman like Nevins's own vulnerability. To hang on to her position, she has to appear that much more confident, aggressive, and unconflicted about her choices—she has to do everything Fred Astaire does, backward, in heels.

Women who've wanted to be perceived as power-ful have long found it more efficient to identify with men than to try and elevate the entire female sex to their level. The writers Mary McCarthy and Elizabeth Hardwick were famously contemptuous of "women's libbers," for example, and were untroubled about striving to "write like a man." Some of the most glam-orous and intriguing women in our history have been compared to men, either by admirers or detractors. One of poet Edna St. Vincent Millay's many lovers, the young editor John Bishop, wrote to her in a letter, "I think really that your desire works strangely like a man's." In an August 2001 article for *Vanity Fair,* Hillary Clinton's biographer Gail Sheehy commented that "from behind, the silhouette of the freshman sen-ator from New York looks like that of a man." A high school classmate of Susan Sontag's told her biogra-phers Carl Rollyson and Lisa Paddock that young "Sue" maintained a "masculine kind of indepen-dence." Judith Regan, the most feared and famous ex-ecutive in publishing—and the woman who brought us Jenna Jameson's best-selling memoir—is fond of bragging, "I have the biggest cock in the building!" at editorial meetings (and referring to her detractors as "pussies"). There is a certain kind of woman—tal-ented, powerful, unrepentant—whom we've always found difficult to describe without some version of the phrase "like a man," and plenty of those women have never had a problem with that. Not everyone cares that this doesn't do much for the sisterhood.

Raunch provides a special opportunity for a woman who wants to prove her mettle. It's in fashion, and it is something that has traditionally appealed exclusively to men and actively offended women, so producing it or participating in it is a way both to flaunt your coolness and to mark yourself as different, tougher, looser, funnier—a new sort of loophole woman who is "not like other women," who is instead "like a man." Or, more precisely, like a Female Chauvinist Pig.

Sherry, Anyssa, and Rachel are a trio of friends who share a taste for raunch: *Maxim,* porn, Howard Stern, *Playboy,* you name it. All three are in their late twenties and, on the night we met, they had recently returned to New York City from a post-collegiate spring break. Rachel, a registered nurse, a tough, compact girl with short red hair, had brought the others a memento: a postcard picturing a woman's tumescent breasts against a background of blue sky with the words *Breast wishes from Puerto Rico!* scrawled in loopy cursive across the top.

"When I first moved to New York, I couldn't get over Robin Byrd," said Rachel. She was talking about New York City's local-access television sex queen. Byrd has been on cable since 1977, hosting a show in which male and female performers strip and plug their upcoming appearances in clubs or magazines or porn movies. The finale of each show is Byrd—herself a former adult film performer—going around and licking or fondling each of her guest's breasts or genitals. "I wouldn't go out till I watched Robin Byrd, and when I did go out, I would talk about Robin Byrd," Rachel said. "Watching Robin Byrd doesn't turn me on, though. It's for humor."

"Yeah, it's all comical to me," Sherry agreed. Sherry had just completed her first day at a new job as an advertising account executive, and Rachel gave her a little congratulatory gift: a thick red pencil with a rubber Farrah Fawcett head smiling on one end.

All three of them loved *Charlie's Angels* growing up, but more recently they had become "obsessed" with Nevins's show *G-String Divas*. "The other day we were on the subway and I wanted to dance on the pole in the middle," said Anyssa. "I could never be a stripper myself, but I think it would be so sexually liberating." Her looks were not holding her back. Anyssa was a Stradivarius . . . a built, beautiful young woman with milky skin and silky hair and a broad, lipsticked mouth. She aspired to be an actress, but in the meantime she was working at a bar near Union Square. "When I'm bartending, I don't dress up though," she said. "Because I have to deal with enough assholes as it is. In college, Sherry and I, by day we would wear these guy outfits, and then at night we'd get dressed up, and people would be like, *Oh my God!* It's like a card . . . you pull out the hot card and let them look at you and it takes it to a whole different level." Anyssa smiled. "And maybe you get to *feel* like a stripper does."

Everyone was quiet for a moment, savoring that possibility.

I suggested there were reasons one might not want to feel like a stripper, that spinning greasily around a pole wearing a facial expression not found in nature is more a parody of female sexual power than an expression of it. That did not go over well.

"I can't feel bad for these women," Sherry snapped. "I think they're asking for it."

Sherry considered herself a feminist. "I'm very pro-woman," she said. "I like to see women succeed, whether they're using their minds to do it or using their tits." But she didn't mind seeing women fail, either, if they weren't using both effectively. She liked the Howard Stern show, for example, because his is a realm in which fairness of a sort pervades: Women who are smart and funny like Sherry, or Stern's sidekick, the FCP Robin Quivers, get to laugh along with the boys. (Quivers has always been the mitigating presence that saves Stern's shows from being entirely frightening. His trademark shtick, getting female guests to take off their clothes so his staff can ogle or mock them, would seem a lot creepier if Quivers—a smart, articulate, fully clothed black woman—wasn't there to reassure the viewer or listener that there was a way out, an alternate role for a woman on the show. But then, Quivers is pretty much the only one who gets that option—the other women Stern invites into his universe are either hot or crazy or, his favorite, both.) The women who are pathetic enough to go on national television and strip down to their underwear in the hopes that Howard will buy them a boob job are punished with humiliation. Sherry and her friends found something about this routine reassuring. They seemed satisfied by what they experienced as justice being meted out; it was like the pleasure some people get watching the police throw the bad guys against the hood of their cars on *Cops*.

"Yeah, we're all women, but are we supposed to band together?" said Anyssa. "Hell, no. I don't trust women. Growing up, I hung out with all guys . . . these are the first girls I ever hung out with who had the same mentality as me and weren't going to starve themselves and paint their nails every fucking second. I've never been a girly-girl, and I've never wanted to compete in that world. I just didn't fit in."

Anyssa is not different from most FCPs: They want to be like men, and profess to disdain women who are overly focused on the appearance of femininity. But men seem to like those women, those girly-girls, or like to look at them, at least. So to *really* be like men, FCPs have to enjoy looking at those women, too. At the same time, they wouldn't mind being looked at a little bit themselves. The task then is to simultaneously show that you are not the same as the girly-girls in the videos and the Victoria's Secret catalogs, but that you approve of men's appreciation for them, and that possibly you too have some of that same sexy energy and underwear underneath all your aggression and wit. A passion for raunch covers all the bases.

Twenty-two-year-old Erin Eisenberg, a city arts administrator, and her little sister Shaina, a student at Baruch College, kept a stack of men's magazines—*Playboy, Maxim, FHM*—on the floor of the bedroom they still shared in their parents' apartment. "A lot of times I say, Oh, she looks good, or check out that ass, but sometimes I'm also like, This is so airbrushed, or Oh, her tits are fake or whatever," said Erin. "I try not to be judgmental, but sometimes it's there."

"I pick up *Playboy* because I want to see who's on the cover," said Shaina. "The other day Shannen Doherty was on one and I just wanted to see what her breasts looked like."

The magazines and raunch culture in general piqued their curiosity and provided them with inspiration. Erin said, "There's countless times in my life where I know I've turned people on just by showing off." By putting on a little performance, making out with another girl, for instance. "It moved into Oh, this turns guys on if you do it in public. Having had that experience in a real-life setting, it was almost as if I was on *The Man Show* or something like that. But those times, it wasn't as sexy as in my fantasies."

Both Eisenberg sisters said they were "not easily offended," and Erin felt she had "a higher tolerance for sexual harassment" than most women.

"I went out with my friend a couple weeks ago and some guy touched her ass and she flipped out at him," said Shaina. "I was just like, Dude, he slapped your ass. To me that would be no big deal—if anything, I'd be flattered."

"You have to understand, a man is a man; it doesn't matter what position he's in," Erin said. "I have a lot of male friends. I feel conflicted being a woman, and I think I make up for it by trying to join the ranks of men. I don't think I have a lot of feminine qualities."

"You're not a girly-girl," Shaina cut in. "Like, her priority is not, *Am I gonna go get a manicure?*"

"Girly-girl" has become the term women use to describe exactly who they do not want to be: a prissy sissy. Girly-girls are people who "starve themselves and paint their nails every fucking second," as Anyssa put it; people who have nothing better to think about than the way they look. But while the FCP shuns girly-girls from her social life, she is fixated on them for her entertainment. Nobody has to wax as much as a porn star, and most strippers wouldn't be caught dead without a manicure. Weirdly, these are the women—the ultimate girly-girls—who FCPs spend their time thinking about.

Like Sherry, Erin Eisenberg professed an interest in feminism, and she showed me her copy of *The Feminine Mystique* to prove it. "But I don't try to espouse my ideas to everyone else," she said. "I'd rather observe and analyze on my own, and then do something else—further myself in other ways rather than start a debate. I gain strength by not exerting that energy."

"Gaining strength" is the key. FCPs have relinquished any sense of themselves as a collective group with a linked fate. Simply by being female and getting ahead, by being that strong woman we hear so much about, you are doing all you need to do, or so the story goes.

Carrie Gerlach, then an executive at Sony Pictures in Los Angeles, wrote in an e-mail in 2001:

> My best mentors and teachers have always been men. Why? Because I have great legs, great tits, and a huge smile that God gave to me. Because I want to make my first million before the age of thirty-five. So of course I am a female chauvinist pig. Do you think those male mentors wanted me telling them how to better their careers, marketing departments, increase demographics? Hell no. They wanted to play in my secret garden. But I applied the Chanel war paint, pried the door open with Gucci heels, worked, struggled and climbed the ladder. And made a difference!!! And I did it all in a short Prada suit.

Gerlach made no bones about wanting to "climb the ladder" so she could enjoy life's ultimate riches, namely Prada, Gucci, and Chanel. The ends justify the means, and the means are "great legs" and "great tits."

"Everyone wants to make money," said Erin Eisenberg, the daughter of a pair of erstwhile hippies. ("My dad claims he was a socialist," she said skeptically.) Where her parents had misgivings about the system, Erin has doubts only about its lower rungs. Gone is the sixties-style concern (and lip service) about society as a whole. FCPs don't bother to question the criteria on which women are judged, they are too busy judging other women themselves.

"Who doesn't want to be looked at as a sex symbol?" said Shaina. "I always tell people, if I had a twenty-three-inch waist and a great body, I would pose in *Playboy*. You know all those guys are sitting there staring at you, *awe-ing* at you. That must be power."

If we are to look for a precedent for this constellation of ideas and behaviors, we can find it in an unlikely place . . . a novel written before the Civil War. Published in 1852, Harriet Beecher Stowe's *Uncle Tom's Cabin* sold more copies than any book besides the Bible in the nineteenth century, and it is still widely considered to be the most historically significant novel ever written by an American author. Since it was first published, Stowe's book has been credited with having an enormous impact on the way Americans conceive of race. During Stowe's tour of Great Britain in 1853, the minister sent to greet her congratulated her by saying "that the voice which most effectively kindles enthusiasm in millions is the still small voice which comes forth from the sanctuary of a woman's breast." (Stowe proudly relayed his words in her travel book *Sunny Memories of Foreign Lands*.) These sentiments were echoed ten years later by

Abraham Lincoln, who famously called Stowe the "little lady who made this big war" when he met her just after he issued the Emancipation Proclamation.

While Stowe inarguably advanced the cause of abolition (and intensified the tensions over slavery that helped ignite the Civil War), she has also been blamed for exacerbating "the wrongheadedness, distortions and wishful thinkings about Negroes in general and American Negroes in particular that still plague us today," as the critic J. C. Furnas wrote in 1956. Stowe created various characters who "transcend" their race—which is to say that instead of acting "like a man" (or trying to), they "act white." One of Stowe's protagonists is a slave character, George Harris, who is light-skinned enough to pass as "a Spanish gentleman." But it is not just the skin Stowe gave him that allows George to move through her fictive society and her reader's imagination distinct from other slaves. In "Everybody's Protest Novel," an essay on *Uncle Tom's Cabin* published in the *Partisan Review* in 1949, James Baldwin wrote that Stowe crafted George "in all other respects as white as she can make" him; Stowe created George "a race apart" from Tom and his fellow slaves.

The converse strategy for coping with race in Stowe's text is the one that has become notorious, and it is, of course, the one exhibited by Uncle Tom. Tom, remember, is a creation of Stowe's who so thoroughly accepts his oppression as a slave, he renders the standard appurtenances of enslavement unnecessary. When a slave trader transports him for sale, Tom can be left unshackled; there is no chance he will run away because he has so completely internalized the system of which he is a victim. He believes that he really *is* property, so to run away would be to rob his owner, a crime he wouldn't dream of committing.

Consequently, Tom is thought of by his masters—and by Stowe herself—as "steady," "honest," "sensible," and "pious." Not only does Tom submit to the system that oppresses him, he actively strives for the love of his oppressor, and loves him in return. George Shelby, the man Tom has served since his birth, is too ashamed to say good-bye to Tom after he literally sells him down the river, thus separating Tom from his wife, children, and home, and condemning him to a bleak and lethally brutal future. Yet Tom's wistful parting words as he is carted off to the auction block are, "Give my love to Mas'r George."

Stowe wanted Tom to serve as a heartbreaking and representative example of the "soft, impressible nature of his kindly race, ever yearning toward the simple and childlike." In her book, this is simply the character's character. But the concept of an Uncle Tom has taken on a meaning very different from the one Stowe intended. An Uncle Tom is a person who deliberately upholds the stereotypes assigned to his or her marginalized group in the interest of getting ahead with the dominant group.

In a discussion of "Tom shows," the staged adap-

tations of *Uncle Tom's Cabin* that became wildly popular after the book's publication (and remained so
into the 1930s), author Mary C. Henderson describes
a "theatrical industry called 'Tomming,'" in which
"Uncle Tom's original character was almost totally
obliterated in the worst and cheapest dramatizations.
Somewhere in tents set among the cornfields he lost
his dignity and his persona and became the servile,
obedient, sycophantic black man who gave the term
'Uncle Tom' its terrible taint."

Tomming, then, is conforming to someone
else's—someone more powerful's—distorted notion of
what you represent. In so doing, you may be getting
ahead in some way—getting paid to dance in blackface in a Tom show, or gaining favor with Mas'r as
Stowe's hero did in literature—but you are simultaneously reifying the system that traps you.

The notions of "acting white," as Stowe crafted
George Harris to, and "acting black," as she decided
Uncle Tom did (thus expressing the "nature of his
kindly race"), are both predicated on the assumption
that there is a fixed, unchanging essence of whiteness
and another of blackness which can then be imitated.
James Baldwin wrote, "We take our shape, it is true,
within and against that cage of reality bequeathed us
at our birth; and yet it is precisely through our dependence on this reality that we are most endlessly betrayed." The cage in which we "find ourselves bound,
first without, then within," is the "nature of our categorization." We are defined and ultimately define

ourselves, Baldwin argued, by the cultural meaning assigned to our broadest human details—blackness, whiteness, maleness, femaleness, and so on. In order to start Tomming, "acting black," we would necessarily have to first believe that there was such a thing as blackness to enact. And likewise, if we are going to act "like a man," there has to be an inherent manliness to which we can aspire.

It would be crazy to suggest that being a woman today (black or white) is anything remotely like being a slave (male or female) in antebellum America. There is obviously no comparison. But there are parallels in the ways we can think about the limits of what can be gained by "acting like" an exalted group or reifying the stereotypes attributed to a subordinate group. These are the two strategies an FCP uses to deal with her femaleness: either acting like a cartoon man—who drools over strippers, says things like "check out that ass," and brags about having the "biggest cock in the building"—or acting like a cartoon woman, who has big cartoon breasts, wears little cartoon outfits, and can only express her sexuality by spinning around a pole.

In a broader sense, both of these strategies have existed historically and continue to because to a certain extent they are unavoidable. Does a marginalized person—a female producer going to a job interview at an all-male film company, a Chinese attorney striving to make partner at an old-boy, white-shoe law firm, a lesbian trying to fit in at a Big Ten keg party—need to act the way the people in charge expect in order to get what he or she wants? Without question. A certain amount of Tomming, of going along to get along, is part of life on planet Earth.

But Americans gave up the idea—or tried to, or pretended to—that there are certain characteristics and qualities that are essentially black and essentially white a long time ago. At the very least we can say that it would be considered wildly offensive and thoroughly idiotic to articulate ideas like that now. Yet somehow we don't think twice about wanting to be "like a man" or unlike a "girly-girl." As if those ideas even *mean* anything. Like which man? Iggy Pop? Nathan Lane? Jesse Jackson? Jesse Helms? It is a staggeringly unsophisticated way to think about being a human being, but smart people do it all the time.

The most obvious example in recent memory of someone intelligent espousing such ideas publicly is the scholar Camille Paglia. Paglia notoriously proclaimed that "if civilization had been left in female hands, we would still be living in grass huts." That may be too puerile a provocation to bother with, but Paglia's more understated articulations of her beliefs about gender echo our still widely held cultural assumption that women are one way and men are another (and that there's nothing wrong with saying so). In an interview with *Spin* magazine (which Paglia liked enough to reprint in her book *Sex, Art, and American Culture*), Paglia defended her controversial views on date rape and assessed her critics:

They have this stupid, pathetic, completely-removed-from-reality view of things that they've gotten from these academics who are totally off the wall, totally removed. Whereas my views on sex are coming from the fact that I am a football fan and I am a rock fan. Rock and football are revealing something true and permanent and eternal about male energy and sexuality. They are revealing the fact that women, in fact, *like* the idea of flaunting, strutting, wild masculine energy. The people who criticize me, these establishment feminists, these white upper-middle-class feminists in New York, especially, who think of themselves as so literate, the kind of music they like, is, like Suzanne Vega—you know, women's music.

SPIN: *Yuck.*

First off, one has to wonder if Paglia has ever heard of Patti Smith. Or Debbie Harry. Or Janis Joplin. Or Grace Jones. It seems as if she has temporarily forgotten even her idol, Madonna (the subject of two of Paglia's essays in that same book). Aren't these people women . . . who necessarily make women's music? Do these women not flaunt and strut and effuse the wild energy with which Paglia is so enthralled? Are they uptight? Uncool?

Reducing "women's music" to something soft and neutered, something guaranteed to make her—female!—interviewer say "yuck," is a manipulative little move. It's a way for Paglia to separate herself from the human characteristics she finds most unattractive—weakness, effeteness, pusillanimity—and to make these things "permanently and eternally" female. (Which, by the way, Paglia *is*.)

Paglia's equation of all things aggressive, arrogant, adventurous, and libidinous with masculinity, and her relegation of everything whiney, wimpy, needy, and complacent to femininity, is, among other things, dopey. We have to wonder why a woman as crackling smart as Camille Paglia would be so unsophisticated in her conception of gender. We have to wonder why a woman as thoughtful as Sheila Nevins—a woman whose entire career is based on the intrepid exploration of complex stories—would have a knee-jerk reaction to a question that positioned her as a member of the female gender.

Instead of trying to reform other people's—or her own—perception of femininity, the Female Chauvinist Pig likes to position herself as something outside the normal bounds of womanhood. If defending her own little patch of turf requires denigrating other women—reducing them to "yuck" as Paglia does or airheads who prioritize manicures, or, Judith Regan's favorite, "pussies"—so be it.

It can be done very persuasively.

Mary Wells Lawrence was one of the first women in this country to start her own advertising agencies, certainly the most successful, and the first woman CEO of a company listed on the New York

Stock Exchange. She stands out as one of the great giants of her industry, male or female. Wells Lawrence came up with the "I Love New York" campaign, which many people credit with resuscitating the city's image during the seventies; she also invented the weirdly unforgettable "Plop Plop Fizz Fizz" Alka-Seltzer ads.

One of her earliest successes was a colorful marketing strategy for Braniff Airlines in the sixties that eventually prompted a transformation of the look of American airports. Wells Lawrence bucked the bland, military style of the times and had every Braniff plane painted a bright color. Then she hired Emilio Pucci to design riotous costumes for the flight "hostesses." One of her ads featured what she called the "air strip," the process by which Braniff stewardesses paired down their Pucci flight uniforms little by little on the way to tropical destinations. Pucci "even made teeny-weeny bikinis for them, an inch of cloth," Wells Lawrence wrote in her memoir, *A Big Life (in Advertising)*. These ads, with their focus on pretty young women in escalating stages of undress, may have been what prompted Gloria Steinem to famously comment, "Mary Wells Uncle Tommed it to the top."

In her memoir, Wells Lawrence returned fire at Steinem. "What a silly woman," she wrote. "I wanted a big life. I worked as a man worked. I didn't preach it, I did it."

How scalding. How convincing. Who wouldn't

pick action over nagging, succeeding over hand-wringing? Who doesn't want a big life?

There's just one thing: Even if you are a woman who achieves the ultimate and becomes *like a man,* you will still always be like a woman. And as long as womanhood is thought of as something to escape from, something less than manhood, you will be thought less of, too.

There is a variety program on Comedy Central called *The Man Show,* which concludes each episode with a segment of bouncing women appropriately called "Girls on Trampolines." The show's original hosts Jimmy Kimmel and Adam Carolla have left; Kimmel now has his own network talk show, *Jimmy Kimmel Live,* on ABC, and both Kimmel and Carolla executive produce *Crank Yankers* for Comedy Central. But when I went to visit their set in L.A. in 2000, *The Man Show* was one of the top shows on cable, and it was getting a lot of attention for its brand of self-described "chauvinistic fun." Thirty-eight percent of *The Man Show*'s viewers were female. It was co–executive produced by two women.

Like Sheila Nevins, co–executive producer Jennifer Heftler was not who you'd expect to find as the wizard behind the curtain of a raunch operation. She was a big woman who wore batik and had a tattoo of a dragonfly on her wrist and another of a rose on her ankle. She described her program as "big, dumb, goofy fun."

"One of the perks to this job was that I wouldn't have to prove myself anymore," she said. "I could say, 'I worked at *The Man Show*' and no one would ever say, 'Oh, that prissy little woman' again." Heftler felt her female viewers' incentive for watching the program was very much like her own for making it. "It's like a badge," she said. "Women have always had to find ways to make guys comfortable with where we are, and this is just another way of doing that. If you can show you're one of the guys, it's good."

The night I went to a taping, there wasn't enough space to fit all the guys who had lined up outside the studio, and a team of heavy-limbed boys in matching green T-shirts from Chico State were pumped to make it into the audience.

Don, the bald audience fluffer, seemed to be looking directly at them when he yelled from the stage, "A few weeks ago we had trouble with guys touching the women here. You can't just grab their asses—you don't do that in real life, do you? [Beat.] Welllll . . . so do I!" The frat guys cheered, but not with the alarming gusto of the man in front of them, a scrawny computer technician who resembled one of the P's in Peter, Paul and Mary. "To the women," shouted Don, "today only, you're an honorary man! Grab your dick!"

Abby, a brunette in tight white jeans, was called up to the stage for her big chance to win a T-shirt. Honorary man status notwithstanding, she was asked to expose her breasts. Abby declined, but agreed brightly to kiss another girl instead. A pert redhead in her early twenties raced up from the audience to wrap her hands around Abby's back and put her tongue in the stranger's mouth. "Yeah! Yeah! You're making me hard," shrieked Peter/Paul. He was nearly hit in the head by the Chico Statesman behind him, who pumped his fist in the air in front of his crotch, semaphoring masturbation.

Soon after, the stage doors opened and out poured the Juggies, nine dancing girls in coordinating pornographic nursery rhyme costumes: Little Red Riding Hood in spike-heeled patent leather thigh-highs, Bo Peep in a push-up bra so aggressive you could almost see her nipples, and, of course, Puss 'n Boots.

They shimmied their way around the audience, and some did tricks on the poles like strippers. After the shouting died down, Adam Carolla and Jimmy Kimmel emerged from backstage, fresh as daisies in matching gingham shirts. "Who knows a good joke?" Carolla asked.

"How do you piss your girlfriend off when you're having sex?" a guy in the back volunteered. "Call her up and tell her."

Then they showed a pretaped spot about a mock clinic for wife evaluation, where a prospective bride was assessed based on her grasp of football and her aptitude for administering fellatio to pornographer Ron Jeremy.

• • •

There's a side to boydom that's fun," Jen Heftler declared. "They get to fart, they get to be loud—and I think now we're saying we can fart and curse and go to strip clubs and smoke cigars just as easily and just as well." As for the Juggies, we are supposed to experience them as kitsch. "In the sixties, Dean Martin had his Golddiggers, and they were basically Juggies," Heftler said, "but the audience wasn't in on the joke. It was just pretty girls because that's what a guy would have. Then it was, you can never have that, you can't show a woman as a sex object, that's terrible. Now we're back to having it, but it's kind of commenting on that as opposed to just being that. The girls are in on it, and the women watching it are in on it."

But after sitting in that audience, I have to wonder what exactly we are in on. That women are ditzy and jiggly? That men would like us to be?

"Listen," Heftler countered, "our generation has gone past the point where *The Man Show* is going to cause a guy to walk into a doctor's office and say, 'Oh, my God! A woman doctor!'"

Her co–executive producer, Lisa Page, a sweet, quiet woman, said, "It doesn't need to threaten us anymore."

The night after the taping, I had dinner with Carolla, Kimmel, and *The Man Show*'s cocreator and executive producer, Daniel Kellison, at the restaurant inside the W Hotel in Westwood. I asked them why they supposed 38 percent of their viewers were women.

"We did a little research," said Carolla, "and it turns out 38 percent of all women have a sense of humor."

I laughed. I wanted to be one of those women. The women at the W were like another species: lush curves bursting off of impossibly thin frames and miles of hairless, sand-colored skin as far as the eye could see.

"It's a whole power thing that you take advantage of and career women take advantage of," Kellison offered. "If you read *Gear* or watch our show or Howard Stern or whatever, you have an overview of a cultural phenomenon, you have power. You take responsibility for your life and you don't walk around thinking, *I'm a victim of the press! I'm a victim of pop culture!* So you can laugh at girls on trampolines." He smiled warmly. "You get it."

For a moment I allowed myself to feel vaguely triumphant.

Kimmel sucked an oyster out of its shell and then snickered. "At TCA," the annual Television Critics Association conference in Pasadena, "this woman asked, 'How does having a big-breasted woman in the Juggy dance squad differ from having black women in the darkie dance squad?' I said, 'First of all, that's the stupidest question I've ever heard.'"

"Then Adam said, 'Let me put your mind at ease: If we ever decide to put together a retarded dance squad, you'll be the first one in it,'" said Kellison, and all three of them laughed.

"What kind of women do you hang out with?" I asked them.

Kimmel looked at me like I was insane. "For the most part," he said, "*women* don't even want to hang out with their friends."

And there it is. The reason that being Robin Quivers or Jen Heftler or me, for that moment when *I got it,* is an ego boost but not a solution. It can be fun to feel exceptional—to be the loophole woman, to have a whole power thing, to be an honorary man. But if you are the exception that proves the rule, and the rule is that women are inferior, you haven't made any progress.

Four

FROM WOMYN
TO BOIS

 If you were to put the last five or so years in a time capsule, womanwise, it would look like a period of explosive sexual exhibitionism, opportunism, and role redefinition. These were the years of *Sex and the City*, Brazilian bikini waxes, burlesque revival, thongs—the years when women learned how to score, or at least the years when popular culture spotlighted that behavior as empowering and cool. Lesbians are women too, and this trend has hit the young gay women's world—"the scene"—with discernible impact. In the scene, the New York to San Francisco back-and-forth migratory ladies' pipeline, sex is taken so lightly there is a new term for it: "playing." In the scene, people say things like, "I played with her," and they go on "playdates."

This freewheeling nonchalance about sex is evident on the Internet. Craig's List, a site that started in 1995 as an e-mail newsletter founder Craig Newmark sent to his friends in the San Francisco Bay area about local happenings, is now a Web site used by millions of people looking to buy things, sell things, and meet each other across the country, and the women-seeking-women section of Craig's List is the scene's favored cyber pickup joint. A typical posting reads: "Looking for something noncommittal? Hi! I am a fun, cute girl, white, with short red-blond hair. Looking for someone who wants to exchange pictures and hook up . . . right away!" It was listed under the heading, "Playdate?"

The sense of esurient sexual opportunism doesn't abate offline. You can feel it at the girl bars in San Francisco; at the Lexington Club, someone has written "SF rocks. I get more pussy than I know what to do with," on the bathroom wall. You can feel it in New York, where on a cold fall night at a lesbian bar called Meow Mix, a girl in a newsboy cap and a white T-shirt with rolled-up sleeves said to her friend, "Some femme . . . just some fucking femme. I met her at a party three weeks ago and I fucked her and that was cool. But now she's like, *e-mailing* me and I'm just like, chill *out,* bitch!" Her chest was smooth and flat: She'd either had top surgery—a double mastectomy—or, more likely, she bound her breasts down to achieve the look. She thrust her forearm in front of her face as if she were rapping as she spoke: "Some of these chicks, it's like you top them once and then they're all up in your face. It's like, did I get you off? Yes. Am I your new best friend? No. You know what I'm saying, bro?"

Her friend nodded and kept her eyes on the blonde go-go dancer in tiny white shorts undulating on a tabletop near the bar. "Bois like us," she replied, "we've got to stick together."

There was a point at which lesbianism seemed as much like a fringe political party as it did a sexual identity. What better way to declare "a woman without a man is like a fish without a bicycle" than to *be* a woman without a man, a woman with other women? "Lesbianism is a women's liberation plot," was how the group Radicalesbians put it when they commandeered the mike at NOW's Second Congress to Unite Women in 1970. The first installment of *The Furies*, a publication put out by a lesbian feminist collective of the same name in 1972, proclaimed, "Lesbianism is not a matter of sexual preference, but rather one of political choice which every woman must make if she is to become woman-identified and thereby end male supremacy." Lesbianism was the ultimate in dismantling the dominant paradigm, resisting the heteropatriarchy, and all the rest of it, and sex seemed kind of secondary.

But in the scene, what you like and what you do and who you do it to are who you are. Sexual preferences and practices are labeled with a great deal of precision. Within the scene, "lesbian" is an almost empty term and "identifying" requires considerably more specificity and reduction, as in: "I'm a femme" (a traditionally feminine-looking gay woman), or "I'm a butch top" (a masculine-identified, sexually dominant gay woman), or most recently and frequently, "I'm a boi."

It is tempting to pronounce the syllable "bwah," as in "framboise," but actually you just say it "boy," the way in years past you pronounced womyn "woman." Throwing a *y* in *woman* was a linguistic attempt, however goofy, to overthrow the patriarchy, to identify the female gender as something independent, self-sustaining, and reformed. Being a boi is not about that. Boihood has nothing to do with goddesses or sisterhood or herbal tea, and everything to do with being young, hip, sex positive, a little masculine, and ready to rock. Even in an entirely female universe, there are plenty of women who want to be *like a man*.

But bois want to be like a very young man. It's no coincidence that the word is "boi" and not some version of "man." Men have to deal with responsibilities, wives, careers, car insurance. Bois just get to have fun and, if they're lucky, sex. "I never really wanted to grow up, which is what a lot of the boi identity is about," said Lissa Doty, who is thirty-seven but looked more like twenty-four when we met for a beer in San Francisco at the Lexington Club, which everyone calls the Lex. She wore a baggy T-shirt and jeans and had gelled her bleached hair into a stiff fin, like the raised spine of a Komodo dragon. "I want to go out and have a good time! I want to be able to go out to the bar at night and go to parties and go to the amusement park and play. That sense of play—that's a big difference from being a butch. To me, butch is like adult. If you're a butch, you're a grown-up: You're the man of the house." Doty is smart, well read, and well educated, and was working as a courier for FedEx because, she said, "I want to have a job where at the end of the day I walk away and I don't have to think about it."

Doty liked to play, and she also liked to *play.* "It used to be if you flirted with somebody, that was it: You were set for life; U-Haul's waiting out back," she said. "I don't know if it's the whole boi thing or if it's a little sexual revolution that's happened where you can go home and have a one-night stand, just like the gay boys. Before, things were more serious: If you flirted with somebody, you better be getting her number and buying that house and getting those dogs. Otherwise, lesbian community is coming *down* on you. Now, it's more . . . playful."

That sense of play, of youthful irreverence, informs the boi approach to sex and to life. "I think non-monogamy is a part of it," said Sienna, a graceful boi in her mid-twenties with close-cropped kinky hair and a face that flashed back and forth between beautiful and handsome depending on her expression. "To me, a boi is someone who doesn't have so much to prove. Bois are kind of dirty. Sexually dirty, but also we're not in the clean, pressed, buttoned-up world . . . we're like little urchins. A lot of us are artists."

Sienna lived at the dUMBA Queer Performing Arts collective in Brooklyn, a place they described on the Internet as "run by a loose-knit collective, usually made up of visual artists, media artists, writers, songsters, dance fanatics, flirty bohemians, political and cultural activists, and otherwise socially boisterous girls and boys." They had sex parties and art shows, and above the bathroom door, instead of GIRLS or BOYS, it said TRANNIES.

When I met her, Sienna was working as a sometime runway model for Hermès and Miguel Adrover and making big, bright collages at the collective. She had recently moved to Brooklyn from San Francisco, where she'd dated "black women who drove Harleys and were college-educated and loved punk rock. Girls who were maybe butch . . . my whole vision about butch got shattered, though. When I first came out, I felt comfortable wearing a skirt and I had a really big afro, so I looked sort of girly. Because of that, I had all these butch girls after me and they were always pushing me to be *more* girly and I'm not into that; I'm not into all that princess shit. I'm from Alaska, where women are all just pretty tough, and I grew up hunting with these sixty- or seventy-year-old women. So to see all these women who are identifying as butch and acting with all this bravado doesn't mean jack shit to me," Sienna said in her low, quiet voice. "I think of a boi as someone who's not trying to put on airs about being masculine . . . someone a little smarter. Basically we threw the term around in San Francisco, and the last couple years I've heard it more here. It's new."

So new that most people—most lesbians—over the age of thirty have no idea what a boi is. Deb Schwartz, a thirty-eight-year-old New York City butch who had been out for fifteen years and had, at various points, worked as an activist for groups like Fed-Up Queers and ACT UP and as an editor at *Out* magazine, said, "It's just wild to me that there's this whole phenomenon out there that is completely news to me. Here I am, a bulldagger of a certain age, and when I first heard the term—recently—I had a conversation with an equally butch friend of mine and she was completely in the dark, too. What's new is seeing these kids who really seem to be striving for a certain kind of juvenilia, not just masculinity. They really want to be kids. This hit me when I saw this girl—this boi, I guess—barreling out of a store in Chelsea in huge, oversize jeans, a backpack, and a baseball cap pulled down low. And she was running as if she were late for the school bus . . . her whole aura was so completely rough-and-tumble eight-year-old that I wouldn't have been surprised if she had a slingshot in one pocket and a frog in the other."

"When you think about teenage boys, [that's] who bois are modeled after," said Lissa Doty. "Teenage boys are sort of androgynous themselves and playing with identity and the world is open to them." When Doty came out in the eighties, militant feminism and lesbian separatism were still at the forefront of dyke culture. "There was this whole movement of *womyn's land* and *womyn building houses on womyn's land* and insulating themselves from the rest of the world," Doty said, smirking. "I felt like I should be a separatist if I was going to be a good lesbian, but I liked guys as people; they were my friends. It was a whole different world from where we are now."

Where lesbian separatists of years past tried to cleave away from men, bois like Doty are more interested in dissolving fixed ideas of man and woman in the first place. "Bois are a little more open and fluid. I don't want to try and speak for the trans[sexual] community, but I think there are a lot of trannybois who are not going all the way, who are not thinking *I need to fit into this gender mold.* They're saying *It's ok if I don't take hormones,* or *It's ok if I don't have surgery. I can still call myself a boi.* That's great. I think it's cool that a label can be so flexible. I like it as a spectrum instead of one specific model."

Being a boi means different things to different people—it's a fluid identity, and that's the whole point. Some of the people who identify as bois simply think it means that they are young and cool and probably promiscuous. Some, like Doty, date other bois and think of themselves as "fags," whereas others date only femmes. Others are female-to-male transsexuals—also referred to as trans or FTMs or trannies—who are in various stages of the gender transition process, ranging from undergoing top surgery and taking testosterone ("T") to simply adopting the pronoun *he*. Consider this posting from Live-Journal, a Web site on which members keep running diaries of their lives for other members to peruse: "So my story reads that I'm a butch (or whatever) living in Minnesota. Mostly I claim the trans label, but it's not my intention to transition to male from wherever I'm at now. I'm surprisingly comfortable in this gray muck . . . it makes life easier when I live it instead of trying to box it up like take-out." Next to the post there is a close-up picture of a young, shirtless person's head and shoulders. The person has freckles and short, messy strawberry blonde hair and could be a male or a female, anywhere between the ages of eighteen and thirty. The person looks happy.

Many bois, including many FTMs, consider themselves part of a "genderqueer" movement invested in dissolving the "gender binary." They don't feel that dividing the world up into men and women or, for that matter, butches and femmes is a particularly sophisticated way to conceive of gender roles. "I'm so against the whole butch-femme dichotomy," said Julien (née Julie) Rosskam, a good-looking twenty-four-year-old documentary filmmaker and the associate producer of Brooklyn-based Dyke TV.

Rosskam, who had been taking testosterone for several months, will correct you if you say "she," which creates an interesting reality: One of the three people in charge of Dyke TV is a "he." Rosskam was getting the money together to have a double mastectomy.

Despite the hormones and the impending surgery and the mandatory "he," Rosskam found the idea that there are two distinct genders and nothing in between constricting and close-minded. "I just feel really defensive; I don't like when people feel the need to put people into categories like that. If you had a line of women we could put them on a spectrum from the most femme to the most butch, but everything in our world is set up as a dichotomy and I just feel like that's so limiting."

The confusing thing, of course, is why somebody would need serious surgery and testosterone to modify their gender if gender is supposed to be so fluid in the first place. But "transitioning" is very popular. The transformation of women to men is so prevalent within the scene they have a name for it: "butch flight." This is to say that women who don't feel the traditional definition of femininity fits them, who in another lesbian era would have considered themselves butch, are more and more frequently thinking of themselves as transsexual, and doing whatever they can to actualize that self-conception medically.

"I've noticed a lot of different levels of trans, and frankly think there are A LOT of confused lesbians out there," an FTM named Ian wrote to me in an e-mail. When I went to meet Ian in Brooklyn's Prospect Park, I had difficulty picking him out of the crowd. I was expecting him to look like the other FTMs I'd met: like butch women with something somehow off. But Ian looked and sounded utterly and seamlessly male . . . a *real boy*, as Pinocchio would say. He had been taking testosterone for eight months, and had undergone top surgery a year before our meeting. "I went to this guy named Reardon up on Park Avenue" for the operation, Ian said. "It's kind of like a hobby for him, doing sex changes. You walk in and there's all these really, really rich women in there for implants, and then there's me."

For a transsexual twenty-two-year-old—for *any* twenty-two-year-old—Ian was remarkably uncon-flicted about his identity. "I've felt like this since I was three," he said. "I've never felt like a lesbian; I always felt male." Ian's sense of unambiguous manliness is anomalous within the scene. He discovered this when he first arrived in New York City and started attend-ing meetings for FTMs at the Lesbian, Bisexual, Gay, Transgender Community Center in the West Village. "I only did that group on and off because I really had a hard time identifying with a lot of the people in there," Ian said. "Because some people, you're just looking at them and you're like, *Your issues are not in this area . . . you've got issues all over the place.* I mean, the spectrum is broad and gender is fluid or whatever," Ian said, rolling his eyes, "but there are some people who I think are latching onto this term—this 'trans' term and this 'boi' term—and you have to wonder. Like I go on all these Yahoo groups for trans men? And the other day I was reading it and the thing that was being discussed was *Is trans becoming the new vogue thing?* And you have to wonder if it might be."

A butch friend of mine told me recently that for a while, she had been seriously contemplating getting top surgery, as many of her other friends already had. She said, "If you're hanging out with a bunch of trannies it's going to influence you . . . it's like if you're hanging out with people who all have tattoos, you know?" Then she pointed to her tattoo.

Because there are so many people identifying as trans or bois or FTMs, and because these terms can mean so many things, when Ian used Craig's List or other Web sites to meet women, he felt the need to be extremely precise about his identity and his body. "It seems like I have to put it up front, like, *Listen: This is what I am and this is what I've done.* Rather than just saying *I'm trans,* which people could think means Ok, yeah, you identify as male and you probably look like a prepubescent boy and you're running around hooking up. Part of why the boi lifestyle is so appealing to some people is the non-monogamy. There's less attachment, a lot of NSA"—Internet shorthand for a playdate with No Strings Attached. "A *lot* of NSA. There isn't really a commitment issue when you're so fluid."

• • •

Despite all the talk of fluidity and the investment people like Lissa Doty and Julien Rosskam have in reimagining gender, there is another camp of bois who date femmes exclusively and follow a locker-room code of ethics referenced by the phrase "bros before hos" or "bros before bitches," which means they put the similarly masculine-identified women they hang out with in a different, higher category than the feminine women they have sex with. This school of bois tends to adhere to almost comically unreconstructed fifties gender roles. They just reposition themselves as the ones who wear the pants—they take Female Chauvinist Piggery to a whole different level.

Alix, a boi from Brooklyn, said we could meet at an East Village gay bar called Starlight for an interview on a Sunday night. After she didn't show up, Alix sent an e-mail explaining her reasoning: "I didn't see you, but I'd be lying if I said I was there. It was raining and I need to know what I'm getting if I'm going out in the rain for some chick and she better be slammin'. And anyway, I should be the one calling the shots."

During an interview, Sarah, a twenty-eight-year-old market analyst, showed me an e-mail she'd received from an Internet acquaintance named Kelli regarding a femme they both knew from the scene. It read: "I hope she's not a big deal, that you're just riding her or whatever. Do you want me to keep an eye on her? Bros up bitches down." Kelli's peroration was

a play on a catchphrase borrowed from sex traffick-
ers: pimps up, hos down.

Sarah told me she had met "maybe thirty"
femmes over the Internet—on Craig's List and
Nerve.com and through the personals on the Web site
PlanetOut—and occasionally she'd used the heading
"boi seeks girl" instead of "butch seeks femme" just to
mix it up, and because it's the cooler term. But she
wasn't crazy about all of its implications. "I'm not entirely comfortable because so many people I've met
consider boi to mean transgendered or faggot," by
which she meant butch-with-butch or boi-with-boi. "I
definitely do not want my name attached to those definitions. I don't understand the faggot culture . . . I
think it's disgusting," she said, and her face crumpled
with distaste. "What I like about women is femininity," she said. "I'm interested in women who look like
women, who have womanly gestures and smell and
feel, and I don't understand the appeal or the sense of
two faggot dykes riding each other."

Sarah had smooth, icy pale skin and very short
black hair shot with little patches of silver. She was
wearing big jeans and a pinstripe shirt with rolled-up
sleeves under a navy-blue vest, and sat with her legs
wide apart and her big arms crossed over her chest,
making her body a sculpture of toughness. "Femme-
on-femme is stupid to me, too. It's air. It's air on air. It
just seems like Cinemax fluff . . . long nails, you know.
In a butch-femme dynamic, it's not mirror images. One
thing I hear a lot of people say about lesbianism and

gayness in general is that it's narcissistic. I've heard so many people say that, and not just my mother."

Though Sarah's dating MO was fairly lupine, her ultimate aspirations were quite a bit more conventional: One day she planned to give up her swinging bachelor's life and settle down. "I've got this model of a household that's probably sick to a lot of people that makes perfect sense to me," she said. "What I want is to have a job, and have a life, and I want a partner with a job and a life to come home to, and a high standard of living, and I want us to have kids that go to school and do their homework and go on trips with their parents." She smiled for a minute with the self-satisfaction of an athlete about to cream his opponent. "And, you know, at the end of a hard day, I would like to come home from work and have my wife suck my cock."

San Francisco is a good town for bicycles and lesbians. Both roam the streets as if they own the place, as if it were built just for them. Cars and heterosexuals are tolerated. In the area around Dolores Park, there are lesbians with baseball caps, with attitude, with their noses pierced like a bull's, with babies, with Subarus, with motorcycles, with money. As one local put it, "It doesn't matter if you're pink with purple polka dots: If you're gay and you come to San Francisco, you'll find community."

On a warm fall night, Diana Cage, the editor of

the lesbian magazine *On Our Backs* (a sexed-up play
on the title of the longest-running feminist journal in
the United States, *off our backs*), and her friend Kim
were waiting to be seated at an Italian restaurant
about a block away from the Lex. They ran into Gibson, Diana's ex-girlfriend, and their other friend
Shelly, who had just come from football practice for
their team, the Bruisers.

"How'd it go?" Diana asked. She had long hair
and long eyelashes and wore a skirt and lipstick and
toenail polish.

"Football! Hoo-ah!" Gibson said, half kidding.
Shelly, a big girl in a sleeveless T-shirt, offered a dou-
ble-armed flex to emphasize the point. On one bicep
she had a tattoo of a heart with the word "mom"
spelled over it. Diana pulled out a Galois and Shelly
lit it almost instantaneously. "We'll see you later at
the Lex," Gibson said and walked off with Shelly.

Diana watched the butches strut away and said,
"I only date clichés."

When they sat down to eat, Kim was feeling anxious about the evening ahead. Clara, the boi she was
seeing, was supposed to meet up with them later, and
things had been very touch-and-go. "Clara's biggest
fear when we started dating was that I was going to
try and fuck her," said Kim, a pretty, punky twenty-
four-year-old who resembled the actress Rachel Grif-
fiths. She defined herself as "femme of center" but
didn't wear much makeup or jewelry except for a
tiger's-eye stud in her chin. "I find bois the most at-

tractive. I like the young, andro[gynous] look, but I've dated across the board: butches, femmes, trannies. And that really bothers Clara. All her girlfriends in the past have been pretty much straight." Kim offered a rueful little laugh. "It also threatens her that I'm not totally vapid and vain . . . her big relief was when she found out I wear a thong."

"I sort of orchestrated Kim and Clara dating," said Diana. "Clara is someone who I would definitely call a boi, totally, although she wouldn't claim it for herself because she's *too cool.* See now it's like *retro* cool to be butch, because there are so many bois and because of the whole butch flight thing."

"Clara's got this intense thing, her and her friends have a really strong distaste for this whole trans trendy explosion that's going on," said Kim. "But the more I hang out with her the more I'm completely convinced she's a closet trans case: She's obsessed with operating sexually as a male. Completely obsessed. She doesn't make any reference to being queer or lesbian at all. And she sees all of her lesbian traits—either emotional or physical—as completely negative. I've never met anyone who wishes that she was a guy so much." Kim thought about it for a minute and concluded, "Whereas a butch is somebody who is, I guess, a little more comfortable with the fact that she actually *is* female."

"I don't have the patience for any kind of a bros-before-hos mentality," Diana said, "and I associate that with bois. For bois it's like in high school; they're all worried about how they look, and maybe if they have a girlfriend that's not cool, and will their friends approve?"

Kim was looking increasingly forlorn and pushing her pasta around her plate. "This all ties into their kind of approach to women in general—they are so very predatory about it. Clara won't just touch on it like *That girl's hot.* She will talk and talk and *talk* about how she wants to get them home and fuck them." She looked at Diana. "I'm nervous to see her now because I'm not dressed up. And then all of a sudden it's like I'm trying to please a guy. It's like I've come full circle."

Later, at the Lex, a woman in a trucker hat with greasy gray hair and a long, gray Fu Manchu beard was trying to give her dog a sip of her beer. There were a lot of Mohawks and a confusing amount of facial hair on several of the women, and there was a pool table.

Gibson and Shelly were sitting in back, drinking beer and looking at their football playbook, and Diana was on her cell phone with Clara. She snapped it shut and said, "She's being an asshole. She's not coming."

"What did she say?" Kim was crestfallen.

"She's just being an asshole."

Kim went home.

"What did she say?" Shelly asked after Kim was gone.

"She said she wasn't coming here unless she knew she could get laid." Diana's phone rang again. "That was her. Now she's coming."

"I worry about that one," said Gibson, rolling her eyes. "Then again I worry with every twenty-one-year-old I meet that they're gonna get their tits lopped off."

When Clara arrived at the Lex, she looked too young to be in a bar and too small to be allowed on a roller coaster. Diana pulled Clara onto her lap and said, "See, she's nice to me because we're not going out, but if I were your girlfriend I'd think you were a dick!"

The next night was chilly but sweet-smelling and Gibson was riding her motorcycle, whipping around the curves and up the hills. At around ten she went to Club Galia to see "In Bed with Fairy Butch," the burlesque cabaret show a woman named Karlyn Lotney has been putting on since 1995. Lotney is a short, hefty butch who uses Yiddish phrases and has a sort of lesbian Nathan Lane vibe. She gives regular seminars like "Femme/Butch Sex Intensives" and "Dyke Sex: Nuts & Bolts," but she is best known for these shows. She called an audience member up onstage and asked her, "What kind of girl or boi are you into?"

"That one," the woman said, pointing at her date.

"What, have you moved into some weird, monogamous, non–San Franciscan zone?" Lotney asked. She called the date up onstage and the couple made out for several minutes in front of the hooting audience. "Okay! Enough with the processing! Who wants to get laid?" Lotney shrieked.

A gay guy in his twenties came up onstage and agreed to get his first kiss from a woman. "A real dominant one," he said.

Lotney smiled. "Why don't you show him what we're doing these days, ladies?" A muscular girl with a shaved head leapt onstage, grabbed the man, and kissed him with a truly impressive show of ferocity. "Yeah!" Lotney yelled. "This is San Francisco! This is what we do!"

When they were finished, a dancer, chunky and lipsticked, stripped down to her underpants on stage before going into the audience and shaking a dildo at them, which she ultimately put in her mouth.

Gibson headed out into the night.

She pulled her Honda Nighthawk in line with a row of other bikes and went into the backyard garden of her favorite bar, the Eagle, a place that shows gay men's S&M porn on television monitors. She pointed to a dark area behind the cement fire pit. "I had mad sex with this girl there one night," she said. "The next morning I was like, What did I do? How old was she? I ran into her a few weeks later on the street and we went for beers. She was one of these arty types who won't give you a direct answer, but I kept asking her until finally she told me she was twenty-eight. So we had mad sex again. But this time inside."

Gibson said that she would have nothing against settling down. "I keep trying to grow up," she said. "But it never seems to happen."

There are aspects of life in the lesbian community that are distinct and not really comparable to life in the heterosexual mainstream, and of course the young New York/San Francisco scene is only one small slice of lesbian America. But despite the differences between the scene and, say, spring break in South Beach, there are also meaningful similarities in the ways young women across this country, gay and straight, are conceiving of themselves, their bodies, sex, and each other. Women are invested in being "like a man," and in the case of FTMs, women are actually *becoming* men. There is contempt and condescension for "girly-girls" or "bitches" or "hos," confusingly coupled with a fixation on stereotypically feminine women (especially if they are stripping or dancing on tabletops). Elective cosmetic surgery— implants for straight women, mastectomies for FTMs—is popular to the point of being faddish. Noncommittal sex is widespread, and frequently prefigured by a public spectacle: a coed group pumping their fists at the strippers onstage at a CAKE mixer in New York; a drunk girl heeding the call of Girls Gone Wild to show her tits in Miami; a room full of lesbians hooting at a dildo-wielding dancer at "Fairy Butch" in San Francisco.

This isn't about being a lesbian, it's about being a woman. Or a girl.

Five

PIGS IN TRAINING

There's a rumor going around that "rainbow parties" are the latest teen rage. Rainbow parties are good old-fashioned slumber parties, with a distinctly contemporary twist: All the girls in attendance put on a different color of lipstick, invite over one lucky boy, and then one by one they treat him to oral sex until voilà! His penis is a spectral color chart.

Everyone talks about rainbow parties, but no one will admit to actually having been at one, which leads me to believe that rainbow parties are more like unicorns than like typical Friday nights. (Rainbow parties are not to be confused with rainbow *gather-*

ings, which also involve teens, bright colors, and casual sex, but take place in large wilderness areas, usually out West, where there are rock bands and camping and crafts besides fellatio.) If rainbow parties are a fiction, however, the climate in which they are plausible is entirely real.

In December 2002, a middle-school girl performed fellatio on the high school boy sitting next to her on the school bus in Kingston, Massachusetts, while their classmates watched. The same thing had happened with a pair of seventh-graders on a school bus back in 1999 in Talbot County, Maryland, where an eighth-grade girl also fellated her neighbor during a crowded study hall. These incidents may have inspired two thirteen-year-olds in Beaver County, Pennsylvania, who were suspended for engaging in a round of oral sex (her on him) in the back of a school bus during a spring field trip in 2004.

In the winter of 2004, an eighth-grade girl at Horace Mann, one of the top private schools in New York City, made a digital recording of herself masturbating and simulating fellatio on a Swiffer mop. She sent the clip to a classmate she liked, and in a show of gallantry that could come only from a teenage boy, he promptly broadcast the clip to all of his friends. Soon after, someone with the screen name "nyprivateschool" posted the entire thing on Friendster, a Web site where people of all ages can put up their own profiles, link to their friends, meet their friends' friends, and form expanded online communities.

After the digital video went up on Friendster, people started calling the school "Ho Mann" and referring to the incident as Swiffergate. As for the eighth-grader, like Paris Hilton before her, the dissemination of her amateur porn swiftly resulted in a major uptick in her level of popularity and celebrity. "People said they saw her walking down the hallway giving autographs," said a seventeen-year-old senior at Manhattan's Trinity School named Talia.*

"At our senior retreat we all did raps, little skits," one of her classmates added. "One of the lines was: *It was the year of Paris Hilton and the Ho Mann ho!*"

There was more blow job trouble later that year at Fieldston, another elite New York City private school. A white female freshman had oral sex with a black male freshman. He dumped her soon after, and she retaliated by calling him the n-word in an instant message to a girlfriend and saying some other pretty awful things. The girl who received the IM told a couple other people about it, and somebody printed it out at school the next day. It quickly ended up in the headmaster's hands. "Then there was an assembly and the girl gave a written apology which someone else read," said Daniel, a Fieldston junior. "The girl was in school for a day. Then she was suspended. Then the disciplinary committee met and they deliberated for like three hours and then they asked her to leave." She was punished, to be sure, but she was also the talk of the town.

*Pseudonyms are used for subjects under the age of eighteen.

On a Saturday afternoon that spring at a shopping mall in Connecticut called the Stamford Town Center, I asked some teens if they could imagine similar incidents occurring at their own schools. Alexa, a junior at Oyster Bay High who was looking at dangly earrings, said she would "definitely expect something like this." She wore a T-shirt that said GOATS REALLY LIKE TO NIBBLE above a cartoon goat who appeared to be feeding off her newly sprung breast. "In my school, what was very popular was seventh- or eighth- or ninth-grade girls hooking up or having sex, whatever, with junior and senior guys," she said. "Parents kept calling the school, like, why is this senior at my house when my daughter is a freshman? They dressed so provocatively, the guys couldn't really tell how old the girls were . . . all they see is a hot girl."

Like a lot of teens, Alexa's classmates usually wore "tank tops with little Abercrombie skirts," she said. "I call them belts because they're so short they might as well be." As if on cue, a trio in tanks and belts came giggling out of the store Forever 21. Two of them said they were twelve, the third was thirteen. Everybody said they wore thongs. (The thong is a literal byproduct of the sex industry. In 1939, New York City mayor Fiorello La Guardia insisted that the city's exotic dancers cover their genitals for the World's Fair, and the thong was born to placate his decree while exposing the maximum amount of skin. Now they are the underpants of choice for pubescent girls.

I saw Hello Kitty thongs for sale at the mall; Abercrombie & Fitch—which markets to seven- to fourteen-year-olds—makes a thong that says WINK WINK and another that declares EYE CANDY; the teen chain store Hot Topic sells a Cat in the Hat thong; Delia's has a little cotton thong with Bart Simpson on the front and another that asks FEELING LUCKY? with a green four-leaf clover stamped on the crotch. The urban youth Web site Dr. Jay's has rhinestone Playboy bunny thongs with matching camisoles. When the *Washington Post* asked Hugh Hefner if he was concerned about his company's attire being marketed to teens he replied, "I don't care if a baby holds up a Playboy bunny rattle.")

Alexa looked pensive. "Actually, I guess something already *has* happened at my school," she said and pulled a folded piece of paper out of her purse. It was a printout of her classmate Jen's blog from LiveJournal, a Web site with over three million users that is extremely popular with teens, particularly teen girls. (It's similar to Friendster in that it is ultimately a way for people to meet, or at least cybermeet.) The printout from Jen's LiveJournal blog read: "I think it's funny how you say: 'i don't need to cry acid tears to get attention, only wear a low-cut shirt' so basically you're admitting that you're a slut? That's what I thought, so shut your big ass mouth that's been stretched out from those 5 dicks you sucked about 10 minutes ago and fucking listen up bitch."

The low-cut shirt-wearing subject of the rant, a

freshman, distributed copies of the blog throughout the school, thus ensuring that everyone knew she was accused of dressing provocatively and fellating promiscuously . . . which is not really all that surprising when you consider that appearing slutty and getting recognition for it (she was suspended) are the fast track to heightened female stardom right now, in high school as in life.

What all of these adolescent incidents have in common are, of course, exhibitionism and oral sex—oral sex for the boys, that is. Like the mythical rainbow parties, these situations revolve around girls giving erotic performances and boys literally lying back and enjoying the benefits. "A lot of guys expect oral sex," Talia said. "Not girls . . . people would think they were weird if they did." (That sentiment was echoed almost unanimously by the fifty young people I spoke to between the ages of twelve and eighteen; there is no clinical data available comparing the percentage of girls versus boys who perform oral sex.) I asked Talia if most girls expected *any* kind of reciprocal sexual gratification for their services. "I don't think most girls are expecting to have orgasms in high school," she concluded, "but most guys are. Oh, definitely."

Jessica, a senior from Southern California, keeps a home page on LiveJournal—a mosaic of pictures of Paris Hilton with the caption, "You are a blonde sickeningly happy and popular, some would consider you flaky as they come. It's probably just because they're jealous of your happiness. I mean . . . you have the looks, the lover, and the popularity . . . what more is there to life?" Besides Paris Hilton, Jessica said she looked up to Pamela Anderson: "i love their style and i have blue eyes and color my hair blonde and watch my weight," she said, via instant messenger. She characterized her social group as sexually active, saying that oral sex was extremely common "especially for guys," but for girls "not so much, i think it may be cuz they're less comfortable with having someone down there." Comparing oral sex to intercourse, Jessica said that "it's not much of a difference" because both are "super casual." "I think these days, people at my age, (around 16/17) are so desperate, they don't really care who they get it from," she concluded.

Part of the reason they are so indiscriminate in their choice of partners is that the quality of these sexual encounters in terms of feeling or meaning isn't really the point. Jessica described sex as something they engaged in primarily for bragging rights. "yeah, i have a good example for you! okay so like every weekend, i get together with a group of friends, guys and girls, and we end up playing this game called 'slut on the bus.' every player puts their hands up and takes turns saying things like 'i never had sex' 'i never watched porn' etc and if the other players have done that thing, they put a finger down. first person to put all ten fingers down wins! 'slut on the bus.'"

These are not stories about girls getting what they want sexually, they are stories about girls gaining acclaim socially, for which their sexuality is a tool. While it would be "weird" for a teen girl to pursue sexual gratification, it is crucial that she seem sexy—raunchy, willing, wild. (That's where the Internet really comes in handy. It allows young women to act out in front of the maximum number of eyes.) The Swiffer sucker and her compatriots at Fieldston and Oyster Bay High weren't so much experimenting with sex as experimenting with celebrity, albeit a cheesy, tacky, rainbow party–esque version—the kind that's the most popular and pervasive in our culture today. As one hipster from the senior class at the progressive, elite Saint Ann's School in Brooklyn Heights said, "There's something so *Girls Gone Wild* about this. Like videotaping yourself giving a blow job to a Swiffer? It seems like the kind of idea you'd get watching bad reality TV." Which, of course, many Americans do: Bad reality TV is the most rapidly proliferating genre on television. You can almost imagine a show called *Slut on the Bus* as the next *Survivor* spin-off. Adolescents are not inventing this culture of exhibitionism and conformity with their own fledgling creative powers. Teens are reflecting back our slobbering culture in miniature.

Life is pretty good if you're David. He already had everything going for him: huge, ocean-blue eyes, a blond goatee, a coveted summer job as a ball boy for his hometown baseball team, the Oakland As, and the pleasant cockiness of a seventeen-year-old guy who is used to things working out. But after a fly ball hit him in the face during a late August game and a clip of the incident was played on ESPN Sport Center, David became a temporary local celebrity. People whom he had never met before started coming up to him to say *Nice play!* and more girls than usual were smiling at him in the halls at school. Not a bad set of circumstances in which to begin your senior year.

"Plus I have a really great schedule," he said over an iced coffee after his first day of classes. "I only have to be there Monday, Tuesday, Wednesday, Thursday. I can go skiing, I can go to Tahoe for the weekend, I can do whatever. And my classes are really cool: We're reading James Baldwin and Tupac [Shakur]. It'll be a great year. So that'll be nice."

David waved every twenty minutes or so at the passing trios of girls in tight, low-rider jeans and tank tops milling around outside the Jamba Juice and the Peet's Coffee and the Noah's New York Bagels that sit in a row on Mountain Boulevard, about a half an hour east of San Francisco. This was in the wealthy part of Oakland, where the cars were mostly Volvos, Saabs, and Range Rovers, within walking distance from Head-Royce, the small, private high school that David and his friends attended. These were teens whose parents paid a lot of attention—and money— to their children's preparation for successful futures. The Head-Royce campus spread over fourteen acres with views of the San Francisco bay, the average class size was fifteen, and tuition for high school students was over $20,000 a year. For fun, they would occasionally go into the city to try their luck at the bars with their fake IDs, and David and his male friends had a "tradition" of going to a San Francisco strip club when one of them turned eighteen. But mostly their social life was local: Mountain Boulevard after school, weekend nights partying at the house of whoever's parents were out of town, the occasional dance, the regular sporting events, the weekly boys' poker night.

"We need a guys' night out, because at a party the main objective is like getting a girl's number or getting with a girl," David explained. "I have a friend who's crazy . . . at the end of the night he's just not happy if he's not hooking up." I asked him if by hooking up he meant actual sex or just fooling around. "It depends," David said. "It's like with some of his regular girls, that will happen."

David said that generally, his classmates were not promiscuous, but that looking loose was the defining characteristic of his female friends' style. "There's not really any sluts at my school, but if you walked in there on your first day, you'd think my whole school was sluts. Everyone's in tight, white pants and little skirts and little shirts. I know girls who've gone on the pill even though they're not having sex just so their boobs would get bigger."

There's a lot to look at if you're a guy, and a lot

of pressure to make yourself worth looking at if you are a girl. David described the typical female getup as a uniform: a slut uniform. "Guys can wear all different styles," he said, flapping the front of the blue polo shirt he was wearing. (In fact, he looked pretty much the same as the male seniors did when I was in high school: sunglasses, cargo shorts, flip-flops. Guy wear.) "Guys try to make a match, but you throw on some clothes and you're just who you are and you hope the girls like you. If guys try too hard, they get labeled metrosexual or gay."

That day at school, David had been sitting on one of the big couches in the hallway at Head-Royce with a friend. A middle-school girl (who was twelve or thirteen) walked by and caught his friend's eye. So she pulled up her shirt, pulled out the strap of her thong from under the side of her skirt, and snapped it at him. "When you see that, your first reaction as a guy is that you think, *That girls wants it.* Wants you. Wants any guy out there," said David. "But honestly they don't. They're just dressing that way. It's not like it used to be where you'd see a girl and she'd be really flirtatious with you and you'd get that signal like, *Oh, she might like me.* Now, every girl is really flirtatious. It seems like girls are trying almost to suck up to the guys."

An example, he said, would be all the lap dancing and girl-on-girl action at school dances. "There's this whole stereotype, and it's probably largely true, that guys kind of like two girls kissing each other. So you'll see a guy sitting on a chair—at, you know, a *high school dance*—and two girls will just go up and give him this huge lap dance and start making out. You see it and you're sitting there thinking, Okay, maybe this is what this girl is into, but probably not because she's been with my friends or she's been with me: I know she likes boys. So I think she's just doing it to appeal to the guys . . . always trying to find this *new way in* to appeal to the guys."

One of David's best female friends, Anne, agreed. "Definitely girls hook up with other girls because they know the guys will like it," she said. "They think, *Then the guys are going to want to hook up with me and give me a lot of attention* . . . definitely. If they think a guy's going to like it, they'll do it."

The transition from being little people focused on playing games to being little people focused on looking lickerish is swift and powerful. Robin, a classmate of David and Anne's, said she was "always the biggest dork in school until sixth grade, when it clicked in my head you had to dress a certain way. It's amazing how fast it happened . . . going from where a couple of my friends still played with stuffed animals to wearing short skirts that barely covered my butt and going to eighth-grade parties. Sexually, we didn't really do anything, but you wanted to *look* like you did."

Robin said that there had been a recent push for a dress code at Head-Royce. "Teachers felt it was distracting for girls to be wearing short skirts and little tank tops; in middle school everyone wears basically their underwear." The proposed dress code was abandoned because the idea of such regimentation was wildly unpopular in the school's liberal East Bay locale. "There was so much backlash," said Robin, "guys said they would come to school in miniskirts to protest." Her own objections to the prospect of a minimum fabric requirement were practical. "They were talking about not having your bra straps showing, which was just ridiculous because with half the shirts that the girls have now that happens. The principal asked me what I thought about the dress code, and [I said] if it happens, all of the girls are going to need new clothes."

It's interesting that the teachers were concerned about *boys* getting distracted. Teenage boys tend to find teenage girls distracting no matter what they are wearing. As David put it, "What girls don't understand is guys *always* want girls. If every girl dressed casually, you'd still like girls. It's like, you don't have to exhaust yourselves." The people who are really distracted by the competition to look and seem sexy are the girls themselves.

The most popular creative outlet for adolescent female energy seems to be the expression of imaginary licentiousness through gesture, demeanor, dress. Of course, teenage girls have long been wiling away the hours doing each other's nails and applying facial masks; the years when puberty sets in and casts its transformative spell on brain and body are the years in which people grapple and play with their new-found sexual powers. But there is now a rigidly specific message girls are required to convey before they even grasp its meaning.

"To dress the skankiest, I know that sounds terrible, but that would be the one way we all compete. Since seventh grade, the skankier, the smaller, the more cleavage, the better," said Anne. "I wasn't particularly sexual then," when she was in seventh grade, when she was *twelve*, "but I wanted guys to want me, to want to hook up with me, I guess . . . even though I didn't want to hook up with them. I always wanted all the guys to think I was the hottest one."

Anne may very well have been the hottest one: She was a tall, tan girl with lovely, light freckles across her cheeks, long limbs, and silky gold hair. Her beauty was made poignant by the way you could still see what she must have looked like as a little girl when she grinned. As we spoke she touched her thin, exposed stomach constantly. "My mom had to say, 'If you weigh less than a certain amount you're grounded,'" Anne told me. Where David was difficult to silence on baseball, books, photography, the merits and drawbacks of small schools versus big universities, and the shape he imagined for his future, Anne seemed to have only one truly engrossing passion: her looks. She expressed interest in becoming a graphic designer and talked a little about the year she had spent on an exchange program abroad. But no topic elicited the same kind of intensity from Anne as her own appearance.

"For me it's all attached to guys," she said. "Like I have this weird link between certain guys and my own self-worth. It's like the skinnier I can be, the more they'll like me. There's this one guy, John, he's David's friend, we went out a really long time ago. Ever since then we've had this sexual chemistry. He never gives me what I want, never shows me that he really likes me, or he does but in small amounts. So I always feel like if I can wear something that he likes or if I can be really thin or if I can do certain things to my physical appearance, he'll like me more."

She had evidence, albeit inverted, to support this idea. "John gets mad at me if I wear sweatpants," she said. "One time I went to Ecuador and I lost a lot of weight and he was, like, *disgusted* by me. He got mad at me because I didn't have an ass anymore. I was in tenth grade."

Anne tried hard to hold up her end of the bargain—to be as hot and to wear as little as possible. Her demand in return was that John reserve his attention for her exclusively. In fact, her aspiration was for boys in general to make her the sole focus of their appreciation. "I remember one time I was at John's house with him and David, and I was looking at the *Sports Illustrated* swimsuit issue," Anne said. "I got in a really, really terrible mood and I wouldn't talk because I thought Heidi Klum was just so pretty, and I was, like, *mad*. I get really upset when guys find girls really attractive. Because I want that attention."

Though she was deeply invested in getting attention for her sexuality, Anne's own experiences with sex had been disappointing. She and John lost their virginity together, an encounter she had hoped would be romantic and "involve a lot of emotion," but it turned out otherwise. "My first time I said that I wanted to be in love and he, like, got mad at me. He was like, Oh, that's not gonna happen, are you kidding me? So then I said, Oh, wait, I don't think I'll be in love; it's okay. I guess I didn't really want to, but I told him I did. He was like, I feel like I'm *raping* you! He broke up with me a week later."

For most of her friends, Anne said, things were similar: Sex was something you did to fit in more than something you did for pleasure. "It's an ego thing. We talk about it like at lunch on the patio; people think it's cool. It's competitive: who can hook up with the most guys and who can have sex, who can be the most . . . like my friend is having her eighteenth birthday party and she wants to have strippers there."

Anne asked me if things were different when I was in high school. I told her that it was the same in the sense that you always wished you could be the prettiest and the most popular, the one who guys wanted to be with and girls wanted to be. But the obligation to present yourself as the skankiest—which means the smuttiest, the loosest, the most wanton—even before you've become libidinous (before you are "particularly sexual," to borrow Anne's phrase), is something new. When I went to high school, you wanted to look good and you wanted to look cool, but you would have been embarrassed to look slutty.

Anne looked at me, baffled. "So how did you get the guy?" she asked. *"Charm?"*

Anne is not making lewd tapes of herself and putting them up on the Internet. She's not doing anything untoward on the back of the school bus. She isn't even snapping her thong at boys in the hall. But performing is still an engrossing part of her life. "I definitely feel like because I've put so much consciousness into my appearance in the past, now I get scared of having a relationship that's actually based on what's inside of me," she said.

Monitoring her appearance and measuring the response to it have been her focal point. If her looks were a kind of hobby—if dressing and grooming and working out were things she did for *pleasure*—then the process would be its own reward. But she spoke of her pursuit as a kind of Sisyphean duty, one that many of her friends had charged themselves with as well.

If girls seem more focused on what is expected of them than on what they want, they aren't the only ones. In her book *Dilemmas of Desire: Teenage Girls Talk About Sexuality* (2004), Deborah L. Tolman, associate director and senior research scientist at the Center for Research on Women at Wellesley College, observed that "in the many hundreds of studies that have been done to determine what predicts adolescent girls' sexual behavior, only a handful ha[ve] identified girls' sexual desire as a potential factor." For understandable reasons, our overwhelming focus on teen sexuality in the wake of AIDS has been on danger and "risk behavior." Tolman writes that "this tendency, an artifact of public policy and funded research geared toward avoiding the risks of sexuality, leads us to single out girls as the receptacle of our concerns."

Again, there is a basis in logic here: Girls are the only ones who get pregnant, and girls can contract HIV more easily from intercourse than boys can. But if our fears for teens and teen girls in particular are justifiable, our response has not been. We are pouring an enormous amount of money into abstinence-only education—that is, sexual education that promotes virginity and discredits or disregards contraception—despite the fact that not a single study has shown this approach *works*. Under the administration of George W. Bush, annual funding of $168 million was allocated for fiscal year 2005 to three federal programs designed to promote abstinence-only education. (Those are Section 510 of the Social Security Act, the teen pregnancy prevention section of the Adolescent Family Life Act, and the Special Projects of Regional and National Significance program.) In total, this country has spent nearly $1 billion on abstinence education since 1996.

Eighty-six percent of public school districts that offer sex ed require the promotion of abstinence, and 35 percent require abstinence be taught as the sole option for unmarried people; both teach that contraception is ineffective or don't talk about it at all. A December 1, 2004, report from Representative Henry Waxman (D-CA) concluded that the most popular federally funded abstinence-only sex education curricula contain distortions of medical evidence and basic scientific facts. There is not a single federally funded program to promote comprehensive sex ed that covers both abstinence and contraception, despite the fact that more than 75 percent of parents would like their children to be taught about condoms, abortion, sexual orientation, how to deal with the pressure to have sex, and how to deal with sex itself, according to a study conducted by the Henry J. Kaiser Family Foundation called "Sex Education in America: A View from Inside the Nation's Classrooms."

What teens have to work with, then, are two wildly divergent messages. They live in a candyland of sex . . . every magazine stand is a gumdrop castle of breasts, every reality show is a bootylicious Tootsie Roll tree. And these are hormonal teenagers: This culture speaks to them. But at school, the line given to the majority of them about sex is just say no. They are taught that sex is wrong until you have a wedding (they have seen those in the magazines and on the reality shows too, huge affairs that require boatloads of

Casablanca lilies and mountains of crystal), and then suddenly it becomes natural and nice.

If you process this information through the average adolescent mental computer, you end up with a printout that reads something like this: Girls have to be hot. Girls who aren't hot probably need breast implants. Once a girl is hot, she should be as close to naked as possible all the time. Guys should like it. Don't have sex.

It's interesting (in a nauseating kind of way) to watch educators struggle to make this message coherent. In 2001, I went to the New Jersey Coalition for Abstinence Education's conference in Plainsboro, which was attended by teachers from the Northeast who needed to fulfill a minimum requirement of one hundred hours of continuing education. Hundreds of teachers, mostly women, were gathered in a huge auditorium inside a massive conference center in the middle of nowhere, sitting through hours of speeches while photographs of garish herpes lesions and magnified roving hordes of crabs were projected on a screen over the stage. (That night, I dreamt I got a rare form of lethal mouth cancer from a particularly passionate French kiss. I woke up anxious and aroused.)

My favorite presentation focused on the misadventures of one Miss Tape. An extremely tall speaker named Mike Worley introduced himself to us by listing his basketball credentials and then bragging that he was a twenty-eight-year-old virgin. (He hadn't yet

met *the one,* so there had been no *big day,* so why
would he have had sex?) He told us there were certain rules he imposed on his dating life in order to
maintain his purity: A movie with friends was always
better than a movie alone, a movie at the theater was
always preferable to a movie on the VCR, and if a
young lady managed to make it back to his bachelor
pad, the blinds had to be open, his halogen light had
to be on the highest setting of brightness, and of
course under no circumstances could she go into his
bedroom. People, teenagers, could tinker with the
specifics when they set their own guidelines, he said,
but the most important thing was to never, ever take
off your pants.

To illustrate his not terribly complex point, Worley called a stocky young man from the audience
onto the stage and then pulled out a length of clear
packing tape. "This is Miss Tape. She looks pretty
good, right? She's tall, right? She's . . . what else is
she?" Worley raised his eyebrows at us encouragingly.

"Thin!" someone shouted out.

"Right! She's thin," he said, and wiggled the
piece of tape so it undulated in the air. "And she has
nice curves!" Worley winked.

"So they have sex." To illustrate the act of coitus,
Worley wrapped the piece of tape around the volunteer's arm. After a few more minutes of make believe,
we came to the inevitable bump in the road when Worley said the volunteer had decided to move on to other
chicks. Worley ripped the piece of tape off his arm.

"Ouch," said the volunteer.

"How does she look now?" Worley asked, holding the crumpled Miss Tape up for inspection.

I fought back the urge to yell, "like a dirty whore?"

If I, as an adult, find this kind of educational exercise unconvincing, shame-inducing, and lame, imagine how well it works to influence the impulse control of the average teenager, who (I like to think) is less rational, less self-aware, and more hormonal. In addition to being laced with misogyny (do you want to be defiled like Miss Tape or do you want to be a nice, clean, thin virgin?), the abstinence-only approach has the disadvantage of being unrealistic. Planned Parenthood has repeatedly pointed out that relying on abstinence is ahistorical; teenagers have been experimenting with sex since the beginning of time. Even if we all agreed that teenagers shouldn't be sexually active under any circumstances—and therefore didn't need to know anything about contraception or disease prevention—they are. The majority of high school students graduate without their virginity, according to the Centers for Disease Control. Eighty percent of Americans become sexually active while they're still in their teens. (If history is any indication, that number will continue to rise: As recently as 1982, that number was only 64 percent. In 1968, the year of the summer of love, it was 42 percent.)

Though sexual activity among teenagers barely

varies across the developed world, the rate of teen pregnancy in the United States is extremely high compared to the numbers in other wealthy countries. According to the Alan Guttmacher Institute (AGI), a nonprofit organization that conducts research and policy analysis on worldwide reproductive health (and is quoted and respected by both liberal and conservative groups), Japan and most western European countries have adolescent pregnancy rates of less than 40 per 1,000. (Uber-progressive Holland shines with only 12 pregnancies per 1,000.) The numbers go up in Australia, Canada, and New Zealand, where there are between 40 and 69 teen pregnancies out of every 1,000. But in the United States, we have more than 80 teen pregnancies per 1,000. Rather than being on par with other nations of comparable privilege, our teen pregnancy rates match those of Belarus, Bulgaria, and Romania. On their Web site, AGI offers a succinct explanation for this fairly pathetic state of affairs: "The primary reasons why U.S. teenagers have the highest rates of pregnancy, childbearing and abortion among developed countries is less overall contraceptive use and less use of the pill or other long-acting reversible hormonal methods, which have the highest use-effectiveness rates. Factors in cross-country differences in teenagers' contraceptive use include negative societal attitudes toward teenage sexual relationships, restricted access to and high cost of reproductive health services, [and] ambivalence toward contraceptive methods." AGI also

points out that "though teenagers in the United
States have levels of sexual activity similar to their
Canadian, English, French and Swedish peers, they
are more likely to have shorter and more sporadic
sexual relationships."

By any measure, the way we educate young people about sexuality is not working. We expect them to
dismiss their instinctive desires and curiosities even
as we bombard them with images that imply that lust
is the most important appetite and hotness the most
impressive virtue. Somehow, we expect people who
are by definition immature to make sense of this contradictory mishmash. Our national approach to the
prevention of sexually transmitted diseases and pregnancy is predicated on the assumption that teenagers
will want so badly to maintain their purity for marriage—despite the fact that half of their parents' marriages end in divorce—that they will ignore their own
hormones, ignore the porn stars on MTV and all the
blogs and blow jobs on the Internet, and do as their
teachers tell them. Unsurprisingly, teenagers are not
cooperating with this plan.

Rather than only telling teens why they shouldn't
have sex, perhaps we also ought to be teaching
them why they should. We are doing little to help
them differentiate their sexual desires from their desire for attention. Many of the girls I spoke to said sex
for them was "an ego thing" rather than a lust thing.

Anne said of her first time, "I guess I didn't really want to, but I told him I did." And hers is not an uncommon experience; about a quarter of girls between ages fifteen and nineteen describe their first time as "voluntary but unwanted," according to the Henry J. Kaiser Family Foundation. The only message that seems to be successfully transmitted to girls about sex and sexiness is that it is something they need to embody to be cool. What's saddening is not that they will end up used goods like Miss Tape or unfit to wear white dresses to their fantasy weddings, but that from the very beginning of their experiences as sexual beings they are conceiving of sex as a performance you give for attention, rather than as something thrilling and interesting you engage in because you *want* to.

To write *Dilemmas of Desire*, Deborah Tolman interviewed two sets of teenage girls, one at an urban public school and one at a wealthier suburban public school, asking them specifically about their experience of wanting, as opposed to their experience of "sex," which so often becomes a conversation about being wanted. She was struck by "how confusing it is to develop a sexual identity that leaves their sexuality out," which was what she heard most of her subjects attempting. Whether or not they had had sex, the girls had remarkably difficult times experiencing or expressing sexual desire. Tolman describes girls who seemed to have "silent bodies," who found a way to ignore or muffle any arousal because they were afraid really feeling it would lead them into the treacherous territory of pregnancy and disease. They could not allow themselves to experience "embodied sexual desire," as Tolman calls it, and, unsurprisingly, they experienced a great deal of confusion and anxiety instead.

Tolman compares these girls to Freud's earliest patients—intelligent, articulate women who suffered "hysterical" symptoms such as the loss of feeling or movement in parts of their bodies because they were so detached from their sexual needs. After (primitive) therapy, their bodies came back to life. Once these women had the opportunity to acknowledge their own sexuality, they could "embody their desire rather than disembody themselves," Tolman writes. Since we are talking about teenagers here, it's important to note that Freud's women didn't have to *have* sex to feel better, they first and foremost had to be allowed to have sexual *feelings*.

Tolman also observed girls with "confused bodies," who couldn't determine if the emotional wanting and physical excitement they experienced was sexual. One girl described being "all hyper and stuff . . . I guess you could say it was a sexual feeling." But it also could have been a feeling of anxiety, or fear, or antsiness. And how was she to know which was which? Sexual feeling was new to her, as it is to all teenagers.

Though these girls didn't experience or had trouble recognizing sexual desire, some of them *had* experienced sex—it was something that "just happened" to many of them. Like Anne, some didn't really want to, but told their partners they did. Others had silent mouths to match their silent bodies and said nothing. Tolman points out that "*not* feeling sexual desire may put girls in danger and 'at risk.' When a girl does not know what her own feelings are, when she disconnects the apprehending psychic part of herself from what is happening in her own body, she then becomes especially vulnerable to the power of others' feelings." Simply put, you have to know what you want in order to know what you don't want.

Tolman isn't suggesting we should encourage teen girls to run out and have sex, she is saying that we should stop focusing all of our attention on sexual intercourse at the expense of educating our children about sexuality as a larger, more complex, more fundamental part of being human. Importuning them to be virgins isn't working; what do we have to lose?

There is another side to this debate, of course, and to try and understand why so many people are resistant to broader sexual education I called Peggy Cowan. I had first met her at the abstinence-only conference in New Jersey which she helped organize in 2001, and when we spoke again in 2004 she had become the president of the New Jersey Physicians Advisory Group. She explained her conviction that adolescents shouldn't be taught about contraception like so: "We don't tell our kids, 'Don't drink and drive but if you do, wear a seat belt.'" Because this is true, and because Cowan is an earnest, polite person, at this point in our conversation I hoped I would be able to respect her perspective and learn from her. "People say 'scare tactics' as if we have an agenda, but my agenda is medical," she said. "One out of four teens has an STD! I had three teenage daughters and I was scared to death . . . looking around, seeing all the pitfalls out there. I had single sex ed and I wish they had that now because it protects modesty; now kids are too comfortable talking about things they shouldn't talk about. I heard of one woman teacher who tells kids how to masturbate. Explaining it! About fantasizing when you shower!"

I asked Cowan if she was against teenagers masturbating.

"I can't say that a young person, when they become sexually aroused, can stop just short of sex."

"Not mutual masturbation," I said. "Just masturbation. Kids shouldn't hear about that? Wouldn't it help them to resist sex?" Is it not, actually, exactly the kind of thing we should encourage teens to do with their very real, entirely natural, impulses and curiosities at a time in their lives when they may well be too young to deal with the ramifications of sex?

"I think that's intimate personal stuff," Cowan said. "I don't know that I have a position on that. No one's ever asked me that question before."

Well, everything to do with sexuality is intimate and personal. But if we are bold enough to cross that boundary to tell young people not to have intercourse, surely, while we're at it, it is appropriate—it is our obligation—to talk to them about how to understand and cope with and enjoy their sexuality. Sex is different from drugs; we can't tell them to just say no and leave it at that. Sexuality isn't something they can opt out of.

Cowan was right that one in four people under twenty-five has a sexually transmitted disease. But, like all abstinence-only advocates, she was puzzlingly unwilling to confront the fact that there is absolutely no evidence to suggest that the promotion of abstinence at the expense of comprehensive education helps to remedy this situation. On the contrary; every single peer-reviewed clinical study on these issues has concluded that the more people are educated, the less they spread and contract STDs.

Clearly, part of the problem is that sex ed in this country has been commandeered by the far right—as has the White House and with it the funding that fuels abstinence-only programs. But if conservatives are averse to any discussion of sex outside of marriage, liberals often seem allergic to the idea of imposing sexual boundaries or limits . . . and simply telling kids sex is fine isn't necessarily any more helpful than telling them sex is bad. Both of these approaches can ultimately have the same result: a silence about the complexities of desire, feminine desire in particular.

One seventeen-year-old girl I interviewed in Oakland (in the most legislatively progressive area in this country) said her mother "doesn't really care how sexy we are. She was really involved in the women's movement, so she thinks whatever you do to feel secure and confident is fine." The tricky thing is that adolescents don't automatically know what to do to make themselves feel sexy or secure or confident. They sometimes have "confused bodies" and they frequently have confused heads. Adolescent girls in particular—who are blitzed with cultural pressure to be hot, to *seem* sexy—have a very difficult time learning to recognize their own sexual desire, which would seem a critical component of *feeling* sexy.

Many of the issues confronting teenage girls are the same ones affecting grown women: the prioritizing of performance over pleasure; a lack of freedom to examine their own varied, internal desires; an obligation to look as lewd as possible. (A few days after the 2004 presidential election, Paris Hilton was on the red carpet at P. Diddy's birthday party at Cipriani, lifting up the voluminous skirt of her pink gown and exposing her vagina to the paparazzi, thus outdoing her friend Tara Reid, who accidentally exposed a nipple to photographers at that same party. All I could think of was Anne's comment: "To dress the skankiest . . . that would be the one way we all compete.") But whereas older women were around for the women's movement itself, or at least for the period when its lessons were still alive in the country's collective memory, teenage girls have only the here and now. They have never known a time when "ho" wasn't part of the lexicon, when sixteen-year-olds didn't get breast implants, when porn stars weren't topping the best-seller lists, when strippers weren't mainstream. (The April 2005 issue of *Harper's* magazine reported that a Palo Alto middle school had a career day in which a speaker touted stripping as a profession.) None of this can possibly be "ironic" for teens because it's their whole truth—there's no backdrop of idealism to temper these messages. If there's a way in which grown women are appropriating raunch as a rebellion against the constraints of feminism, we can't say the same for teens. They never had a feminism to rebel against.

Six

SHOPPING FOR SEX

One of the earliest promos for the HBO series *Sex and the City* pictured Carrie, the bubbly protagonist played by Sarah Jessica Parker, in a postcoital flush next to a handsome guy in bed. He looked bewildered when she got up to go and told him, "I'll give you a call . . . maybe we can do it again some time." Another clip in that same promo showed Carrie drinking with her friends at a boisterous, brightly colored club. Samantha, the brassy sexual enthusiast played by Kim Cattrall, told them, "You can bang your head against the wall and try and find a relationship or you can say *screw it* and go out and have sex like a man."

This promo amounted to *Sex and the City*'s thesis statement. Audiences were captivated. The show
became a Sunday night ritual for 10.6 million Americans, and Carrie Bradshaw became a household
name. The cast of *Sex and the City* appeared on the
August 28, 2000, cover of *Time* magazine, staring out
seductively above the words *Who Needs a Husband?*
People were alternately thrilled and appalled to hear
women talking about masturbation, female ejacula-
tion, and the taste of sperm on a sitcom. The conservative pundit Ann Coulter wrote in 2000, "This is
not how women talk. This is how some men might
talk—if women would let them." Others complained
that the casual sex the characters engaged in was
really more representative of life in the gay community, of which *Sex and the City*'s creator, Darren Star,
and executive producer, Michael Patrick King, are
members. But to me, *Sex and the City* always felt like
a pretty realistic reflection of heterosexual, recre-
ational New York: cocktails, self-involvement, shag-
ging.

Little by little, the show became less about
women having "sex like men" and more about the
characters trying to negotiate their independence as
they pursued intimacy with lovers, husbands, children, and each other. That's how the show grew and
became so good. How many episodes could you
really have watched about women using men for sex?
It's a narrative dead end. So the characters and their
stories became increasingly layered, and there were

subplots about cancer and abortion and divorce and religious conversion.

The spirit of the show remained consistent, however, because the truly defining pursuit of their world wasn't sex so much as it was consumption. *Sex and the City* romanticized the weather in Manhattan, the offices of *Vogue* magazine, the disposable income of the average journalist, but what it romanticized the most was accumulation. There was as much focus on Manolo Blahniks and Birkin bags as there was on blow jobs. Buying things became a richly evocative experience as seen through the lens of *Sex and the City* . . . a feathery pair of mules became the linchpin of a glamorous, romantic evening in Central Park. It was as though without the shoes, everything else— the moonlight, the trees, the man—would dissolve into the night, leaving nothing but the bleak mundanity of regular life in its place.

Another episode was devoted to the reclamation of a lost pair of silver stilettos that represented, to Carrie, her freedom and worth as a single person. The shoes were accidentally or intentionally taken from Carrie at a friend's baby shower. When that friend balked at replacing the $485 sandals, the episode became not about etiquette or excess but about "choice." Was Carrie's choice to be single—and inextricably, somehow, to wear $485 shoes—less meaningful than her friend's choice to be a wife and mother? In that episode, titled "A Woman's Right to Shoes," as in many others, acquisition was the ulti-

mate act of independence. One of the reasons the series was such a big hit was that it accurately reflected
the vertiginous gobbling—of cocktails, of clothing, of
sex—that was the status quo for American women of
means by the turn of the millennium. Carrie sailed
around town with shopping bags on her arm, a con-
dom in her purse, and a little gold Playboy bunny
pendant twinkling on her neck.

The ethos of the show was all about women getting themselves the best and the most, sexually and
materially. They were unapologetically selfish, and
civic-mindedness was scoffed at. Carrie didn't vote; in
one episode Samantha told another character, "I
don't believe in the Republican party or the Democratic party . . . I just believe in parties." The only time in
the series Carrie was confronted with the prospect of
doing something for charity, she dismissed the idea
as ludicrous. (A do-gooder asked if Carrie would consider teaching writing to disadvantaged students and
Carrie snapped, "I write about sex. Is that something
they'd like to learn, these kids, writing about blow
jobs?") *Sex and the City*'s idea of giving back was
more in line with the Bush Administration's prescrip-
tion to the nation after 9/11: The best thing you can
do for your fellow man and your country is to shop
till you drop.

Sex and the City told a hugely influential story
about women, with every bit as much cultural power
as shows like *That Girl* and *The Mary Tyler Moore
Show*. The opening sequence culminated with Carrie

twirling on the street, much like Marlo Thomas and Mary Tyler Moore had before her, and she became a similar kind of pop role model. *Sex and the City* offered a complete lifestyle package—what to wear, where to eat, when to drink (always), who to have sex with—for the high-end, urban liberated woman. But if *Sex and the City* was a deeply seductive feminist narrative, it was also a deeply problematic one, one that articulated many of the corruptions of feminism we have been contemplating.

Like Female Chauvinist Pigs, *Sex and the City* divided human behavior into like a man's or like a woman's. Instead of being a confident woman, Samantha had the "ego of a man." When Charlotte decided to make two dates in one night she was "turning into a man," but when she worried whether she would be able to eat two meals in a row, "just like that, she was a woman again." As is the case within the scene of young New York and San Francisco lesbians, the fantasy Manhattan of *Sex and the City* was a sphere in which sex was just another commodity, something to be acquired rather than shared, so sexual encounters often ended with someone feeling like a conqueror and someone feeling compromised. Rather than the egalitarianism and satisfaction that was feminism's initial promise, these sexual marketplaces offer a kind of limitless tally. Like the teenagers who put the cart before the horse and want to "get" sex before they feel desire, the protagonist of *Sex and the City* often thought more about the way she was experienced than about what she was experiencing. She usually "couldn't help but wonder" what was going on in the head of the man she was seeing, and rarely evaluated her own happiness as such. In an early episode she said, "I actually catch myself *posing*" around her love interest, Mr. Big; "it's exhausting." The idea of women measuring men's interest instead of thinking about their own satisfaction lived on after *Sex and the City* went off the air in a best-selling self-help book called *He's Just Not That Into You* (2004), authored by a former writer and consultant of the show. This book, which Oprah Winfrey called "true liberation" and felt "should be on every woman's night table," displayed in its very title a prioritizing of mind-reading over feeling. "Many women have said to me, 'Greg, men run the world,'" writes author Greg Behrendt. "Wow. That makes us sound pretty capable. So tell me, why would you think we were incapable of something as simple as picking up the phone and asking you out? You seem to think at times that we're 'too shy' or we 'just got out of something.' Let me remind you: Men find it very satisfying to get what they want. (Particularly after a difficult day of running the world.) If we want you, we will find you." Women generally find it pretty satisfying to get what they want too, but *He's Just Not That Into You* is not about what women want. It's about becoming better discerners of what men want. (And somehow that is true women's liberation.) *Sex and the City* was great entertainment, but it was a flawed guide to empowerment, which is how many women viewed it.

On the occasion of the thirtieth anniversary of Nancy Friday's groundbreaking collection of women's sexual fantasies, *My Secret Garden*, there was a panel discussion called "Sex and What Women Want Now" at the 92nd Street YMHA in New York City. The event was moderated by Friday's husband, Norman Pearlstein, the editor-in-chief of Time, Inc.; and besides Friday herself, the other panelists included Candace Bushnell, the author of the book *Sex and the City*, on which the HBO series was based; Candida Royalle; and Faye Wattleton, president of the Center for the Advancement of Women (and formerly the first African-American head of Planned Parenthood). The tone of their conversation was sassy and flip.

"I always tell people, if you have this marvelous sexual fantasy, think twice before you tell your partner," said Friday, who had a devilish cosmetic glow that evening with her red lips, red nails, and reddish-hued eye shadow. "If you care this much about them, you should know if they really want to hear that your great fantasy is to have three men take you at one time!"

"All I can say is I hope you can, because when you do it really bonds you," said Royalle.

"That's the person you should marry!" said the

recently married Bushnell. "In terms of my fantasies, they always have little stories and, like, dialogue. There's actually not that much sex, but there's a lot of dialogue."

"Foreplay!" shrieked a woman from the audience.

"I put the partner in the fantasy," offered Royalle, "but I might have him doing something different, or . . . or in funny hats."

"Doesn't everyone here agree that it doesn't really matter?" Friday asked. "If it takes you where you want to go, if it helps you reach orgasm, does it matter who you're thinking about?"

Wattleton said, "I'd rather like to know that he's thinking about *me* when he's having an orgasm."

"Oh, Faye, you're kidding yourself," said Friday with a snort.

Wattleton used a long-nailed finger to flip her dyed blonde hair out of her face and said, "Or maybe I just think I'm that good."

Pearlstein said, "Faye, the Center for the Advancement of Women just interviewed over three thousand women about gender roles. I was interested that in your study, you asked a question about women's feelings about having a man in their lives, and you asked how important is it to have a man to do the following: be your companion, give you love and affection, to have a family with, to give you physical protection, to do physically demanding work around the house, to support you financially, to make major household decisions. But you didn't ask 'to have sex with,' and I'm curious why."

Wattleton smiled, as if it were no big deal, and said, "Maybe our very own questionnaire reflects the limitations of how far we have gone."

About a year later, Wattleton was a talking head on an HBO documentary called *Thinking XXX*, about the making of photographer Timothy Greenfield-Sanders's book *XXX: 30 Porn-Star Portraits*. She declared, "The fantasy of the porn star is the ultimate fantasy because it's a sexual fantasy. I think that's why it's so disturbing to people, because it really does defy our capacity to control it."

I find it interesting that a person who didn't ask a single question about sex in the "first comprehensive study ever conducted of women's opinions across the board" (as her publicist billed it) feels qualified to make a pronouncement on our "ultimate fantasy." (I am also baffled by the explanation that what qualifies the "fantasy of the porn star" as the "ultimate fantasy" is that it is a "sexual fantasy." There are lots of sexual fantasies; they can't *all* be the ultimate.) But mostly I am disturbed, to use Wattleton's word, by the assertion—from a career feminist—that the only problem with the cultural dominance of the porn-star fantasy is that it defies control.

Porn stars are quite firmly under various controls. Most obviously, they are under corporate control. The adult entertainment industry is valued at between $8 billion and $15 billion, and the bulk of the profits go to the mainstream corporate hosts of whatever service is being provided—Time Warner makes money off of pay-per-view porn, as do hotel giants like Marriott and Hilton; phone companies profit from explicit chat lines; and so on. Any porn star will tell you she doesn't get a fair share of the money her body makes. Of course, lots of people who make popular culture don't feel they get a big enough piece of the pie, from the cast of *Friends* (who famously demanded $1 million, per actor, per episode, because, after all, without them there was no show) on down to me (*I* write *the articles; without me the pages of the magazine would be* blank!). But the stakes are very different for a porn star than for an actor or a journalist, because porn stars are selling something more than a skill: They are giving up the most private part of their being for public consumption.

Sex workers are *workers*. They are having sex, just as strippers are stripping and centerfolds are posing, because they are paid to, not because they are in the mood to. The vast majority of women who enter the field do so because they are poor and have no more attractive alternative. (In fact, the vast majority of women in the field *stay* poor.) For the rest of us who are lucky or industrious enough to make a living doing other things, sex is supposed to be something we do for pleasure or as an expression of love. The best erotic role models, then, would seem to be the women who get the most pleasure out of sex, not the women who get the most money for it. Is a person who has sex or acts sexy because it's her job to really living out our "ultimate fantasy"?

It's a cliché that bears repeating (and substantiating) that most women in the sex industry have been victims of sexual abuse. Unfortunately, it's difficult to find reliable statistics on this subject for two reasons: Women in the sex industry are often reluctant to talk to researchers because of the stigma—and, sometimes, laws—against what they do; and, in many of the studies that do exist, the researchers themselves sound so irate it can be difficult to determine if they are biased extremists or if their outrage is simply the natural product of doing research in a field in which the findings are so frequently heartbreaking. Dr. Melissa Farley, a psychologist and researcher at the Kaiser Permanente Medical Center in San Francisco, says that the vast majority of women in the sex industry have experienced incest or other childhood sexual abuse. Estimates range from 65 to 90 percent, and she is inclined to believe the highest numbers, as are all the other experts I spoke with. Obviously, people who have suffered sexual trauma in the past can move on and enjoy their sex lives in the future. But there is something twisted about using a predominantly sexually traumatized group of people as our erotic role models. It's like using a bunch of shark attack victims as our lifeguards.

Farley directed a study with colleagues from Turkey and Africa called "Prostitution in Five Countries: Violence and Post-Traumatic Stress Disorder," which was presented to the American Psychological Association in 1998. Farley and her team interviewed 475 sex workers and, using the same criteria developed by scientists who study long-term health in the military, concluded that two-thirds suffered from post-traumatic stress disorder (PTSD). That number is twice as high as the percentage of Vietnam vets with PTSD. Farley's team found that the severity of the symptoms—emotional numbness, recurrent nightmares, and flashbacks—was more extreme among the sex workers than it was among treatment-seeking veterans. About two-thirds of the prostitutes studied complained of serious medical problems (very few of which were related to sexually transmitted diseases).

To Farley, there is no significant difference between prostitutes and porn stars. "Pornography is a specific form of prostitution, in which prostitution occurs and is documented. For its consumers, including the mainstream media, pornography is often their original experience of prostitution," Farley writes in the preface to a collection of research articles she edited called *Prostitution, Trafficking, and Traumatic Stress* (2003). Farley, who also considers stripping to be a kind of prostitution, goes on to write, "prostitution today is a toxic cultural product, which is to say that all women are socialized to objectify themselves in order to be desirable, to act like prostitutes, to act out the sexuality of prostitution."

If this seems extreme, keep in mind that we can

learn some of the same things from a very different book by a very different author: *How to Make Love Like a Porn Star*, the memoir of the exalted spokeswoman of the sex industry, Jenna Jameson. Like Farley, Jameson suggests that the sex industry is fluid, in the sense that porn, stripping, and posing nude are, if not interchangeable, then at least interconnected. Appearing in *Penthouse* makes you a more appealing candidate to perform in an adult film; appearing in adult films means you can "headline" at strip clubs— "many strippers get into porn solely because they want to up their rates," Jameson writes. Like Farley, Jameson thinks that women outside the sex industry have internalized its spirit and model their sexuality on porn. The title of Jameson's book, *How to Make Love Like a Porn Star*, indicates that hers is a sexuality worth imitating, and she is proud, she writes, that "more women come up to me with thoughtful praise than men." Jameson tells us that "being in the industry can be a great experience" because "you can actually become a role model for women."

Yet, like Farley, Jameson presents life in the industry as marked by violence and violation: She tells us she was beaten unconscious with a rock, gang-raped, and left for dead on a dirt road during her sophomore year of high school; she was life-threateningly addicted to drugs before she was twenty; she was beaten by her boyfriend and sexually assaulted by his friend. She also writes, "To this day, I still can't watch my own sex scenes."

Of course, Jameson comes to a very different conclusion than Farley. She writes, "Though watching porn may seem degrading to some women, the fact is that it's one of the few jobs for women where you can get to a certain level, look around, and feel so powerful, not just in the work environment but as a sexual being. So, fuck Gloria Steinem." One has to wonder how she puts it together this way. If she feels so powerful as a sexual being, why can't she watch her own sex scenes? If her work environment is so satisfying, why does she say that if she had a daughter, she would lock her in the house before she'd let her get involved in the sex industry? Why does she refer to her vagina as a "ding-ding"? I'm not sure any of this is Gloria Steinem's fault.

Jameson, like most employees of the sex industry, is not sexually uninhibited, she is sexually damaged. She has had the grim misfortune to be repeatedly and severely traumatized, which she tells us plainly enough. Non-coincidentally, she tends to describe her sexual encounters as carnivorous, dissociated exchanges of power. "Sexuality became a tool for so much more than just connecting with a boy I was attracted to," she writes. "I realized it could serve any purpose I needed. It was a weapon I could exploit mercilessly." Not once in that description of her sexuality does she use the word *pleasure*. What Jameson is describing is the true enactment of sex as a commodity, a currency to be exchanged for other things. It is only one of the millions of ways there are to have sex, and from her assessment, it doesn't sound like a particularly fun one. It doesn't sound hot or wild or out of control, it sounds like a relentless routine. It sounds like a job.

Contrary to what Faye Wattleton said, it is opening our minds to the possibility—the reality—that lust and sexiness and pleasure are smoldering away everywhere, always, in an infinite number of ways which in fact "really does defy our capacity to control it." If we were to acknowledge that sexuality is personal and unique, it would become unwieldy. Making sexiness into something simple, quantifiable makes it easier to explain and to market. If you remove the human factor from sex and make it about stuff—big fake boobs, bleached blonde hair, long nails, poles, thongs—then you can sell it. Suddenly, sex requires shopping; you need plastic surgery, peroxide, a manicure, a mall. What is really out of commercial control is that you still can't bottle attraction.

In that same HBO documentary, *Thinking XXX*, Wattleton went on to say, "We all think that we somehow come here fully equipped to enjoy sexuality in all of its explicitness, but you know we really do need a lot of instruction. Just like we need to be taught how to eat properly, how to dress properly—every aspect of our lives we take lessons and we educate ourselves."

Somehow, people have been figuring out how to have sex since the beginning of time. It is not something we need to be taught and sold, because we have our own desires to guide us. Wattleton's analogy is a good one though, because really, you can't teach someone how to eat or how to dress, either. You can teach someone how to use a knife and fork. You can teach someone not to wear white after Labor Day. But ultimately, the pleasure we glean from eating or dressing up or having sex isn't derived from learning rules or techniques, it's based on identifying and satisfying tastes. Cravings.

My father taught me that chopped liver is a delicacy—part of our cultural heritage, something to be savored on festive occasions. To me it will always be smelly cement. But I have always liked anchovies, which not everybody does. I like wearing green, because it suits my skin tone and my self-image. Likewise, certain themes have run through my sexual fantasies since I was very young, just as they now run through my bed. Nobody had to teach me how to want these things, or how to get them.

Wattleton is right that one way we discover that we like plums or cashmere or oral sex is by being exposed to them. But there is a problem with using porn as a tool for mind expansion. You can see almost any sexual act imaginable if you spend enough time on the Internet, but no matter how much porn you watch you will end up with a limited knowledge of your own sexuality because you still won't know how these things *feel*. That will depend on who you do them with, what kind of mood you're in when you do, whether you feel safe or scared (or scared in a good way) when you go about it, and so on. The idea that sex can be reduced to fixed components as it is in pornography—blow job, doggie style, money shot, girl-on-girl—is adolescent: *first base, second base, all the way.* It is ironic that we think of this as *adult* entertainment. I don't see why we should regard porn as a way to enjoy "sexuality in all of its explicitness" any more than we consider looking at a chart of the food pyramid to be a feast.

If *Sex and the City* was a show about women shopping for sex (and everything else) in a proud, new way, raunch culture, which the show alluded to—Carrie wore a Playboy rabbit head necklace, Samantha had a pendant shaped like the mud flap girl, all four protagonists went to a party at the Mansion and met Hef—is about women *selling* sex in a supposedly proud, new way. The two themes, women as consumers and women as things to be consumed, obviously share a common trait: Sex and money are concomitant.

What happens when we put this model into practice? If we listen to our culture and make sex one element of a lifestyle of consumption like the characters on *Sex and the City,* and if we idealize women who sell sex—the women invoked by the charms the *Sex and the City* characters wore on their necks—then what do our own sex lives look like? To what end does treating sex as a commodity lead us?

Iliterally have thoughts like, I've slept with thirty-five people . . . I want to get to a hundred," says Annie, a beautiful twenty-nine-year-old with deep blue eyes and a pale, perfect complexion. "It's such an underlying part of my MO that it's baffling to me when people tell me it's not part of theirs. My friend was saying that she had just been on a first date, and when she was kissing the guy good-night, it felt strange to be kissing someone who was, essentially, a stranger. I kept thinking how strange it would feel to me to kiss someone I really knew. Many of my experiences have been pretty fucking lame, but I'm willing to take that because I want more notches on my belt."

At one point, Annie was really into porn—not as a tool for arousal but as a form of entertainment, a kind of hobby. She bought books about porn stars, read about them on the Internet, even went to see the porn star Houston strip at a club in Manhattan. (She has a souvenir Polaroid of herself, a friend, and Houston in a grinning huddle.) She found porn stars and strippers and the "women [who] have these ridiculous bodies with big orb boobs and long legs with fuck-me pumps" strangely compelling. "They're plastic—literally plastic—like live Barbie dolls. I look at Pam Anderson and I'm like, I *played* with you as a child!" (Barbie dolls were themselves modeled after blonde German sex dolls called Bild Lilli.) "It's fascinating because it's beautiful women doing these crazy things, this demoralizing stuff. Like on Howard Stern, some guy will touch a woman with a pointer and say, 'You need a tummy tuck.' It's humor masking a pretty woman–hating thing—which I've got a good amount of in me, I guess, because I take pleasure in it."

Annie's fascination with raunch culture has been waning, though. "I used to feel like Howard was just this one funny, misogynistic guy who said what no one else had the guts to say, but now it's so pervasive. It's like it's cool to be a stripper, it's cool to be tarty." An interest in these things used to seem like a way of resisting the status quo. Now it feels like a way of conforming.

While Annie has become less intrigued by the selling of sex, she has grown more engaged in sex as a kind of shopping. She described her acquisition of notches as a feeding of the ego more than an adventure into the erotic. "The thing about when you start accumulating sex for its own sake is that the exercise of it is not that sexual." But she said she finds these encounters rewarding in a different way. "It's a way of trying to establish yourself as a kind of woman-man: *I'm not some sad sack, I'm strong and independent and I'm a rolling stone that gathers no moss.* There is something empowering about waking up next to a guy and thinking, I've got to go; what's on the menu next? I used to get so hurt," when it was the morning after the big night, and the adventure had not yielded an enduring bond. "Then, eventually, having a sense of humor and perspective about these things made it so I could wake up and get on with my life. When I felt that switch flip in my head, I thought, Yeah! Now I'm like a guy."

Though there's a way in which she finds these affairs edifying and exciting, Annie said there's also a way in which they can feel "pathetic." "Sometimes, having this kind of sex, this shopping kind of sex, is based in insecurities for me . . . am-I-attractive insecurities." Sometimes, what she really wants isn't sex but proof that she is as desirable, as sexual, as *female* as the Barbie dolls she played with as a child or the porn stars she toyed with as an adult. "It's just interesting to me that I choose to explore sex and sexuality by being willing to have a number of mediocre experiences."

Meg, who is a very successful, very busy lawyer, has been given a nickname by her friends: Sharky. The moniker doesn't refer to her sharklike determination to win her cases or her competitive prowess as a triathlete, but to her remarkable energy as a sexual opportunist. "I hooked up with this guy in Vegas, and it was like I went on a shark attack," she said. "I pretended I was someone else: sweet and innocent . . . *Oh, I never do this! I've never been so turned on in my life!* And it worked. But I wasn't that into him. I think he waxed his whole body."

Meg has strawberry blonde hair and a pretty smile. She sat on the edge of the patio at the Standard Hotel in West Hollywood, dangling her manicured toes in the cool blue of the pool. "I would admit to being a slut, but I'd prefer other people didn't call me that," she said, laughing. "I don't get turned on by monogamy, I get turned on by novelty and the challenge of a new man. Well, I've sort of thought there's this challenge, but I've sort of created it: Men will fuck anyone."

Meg said that she badly wanted to "find a husband. I definitely want to get married, but I worry about how I am going to be in a many-yeared marriage and still get turned on—I'm not turned on after six months." Actually, it didn't sound like she was turned on after six minutes. Meg described her hookups as "usually drunk, usually antiseptic. I think men are turned off by my aggressiveness." But what about for her? Why weren't the experiences sensual for her? "Well, it's not like I love sex; it's not like I'm so into it. It's more like I'm into getting what I want. I guess it's more like I feel like I won."

To say that Lynn is aggressive is sort of like saying Bill Clinton is charismatic . . . It isn't a personality trait of hers so much as a force around which her personality is organized. "The great thing about Miami is that everyone drives so slow it's really easy to cut them off," she said, mashing her foot down on the gas pedal to speed in front of a line of cars. She had moved to Miami only four days before we met, but she seemed to be settling into her new life there, as an events producer, with ease. Lynn has a sweet face, like an illustration from a children's book, and that night it was framed by two brown pigtails. Both of her middle toes are tattooed with stars. She wore cargo pants and a T-shirt over a thermal underwear top, and looked much younger than thirty-two.

She pulled into the parking lot of an Irish dive bar that felt out of place among the flesh-and-salsa clubs that line Ocean Drive and Collins Avenue. Frailey, originally from Dallas, Texas, ordered Bud in a bottle at the bar. "Most of my friends are guys . . . I just think they're easier," she said. "Girls are just, like, girly. I don't wear makeup and I don't blow out my hair. I'm just not into the whole, *Oh my God, did you see the new pair of shoes they have on sale?* It's not that I have anything against all that stuff, it's just that it's not a topic of conversation for me. When I'm with my girlfriends talking about guys I'm like *How big was his dick?* Not that I'm always that crude, but if I'm going to talk about sex, it's just, *Did he go down on you,* not, *Are you going to marry him?*"

Lynn's parents split when she was twenty-six after a marriage of adventure and religion. Her family moved around and spent many years in Morocco, where her parents were missionaries. "My father would preach Sunday mornings in Rabat and then the whole family would load up into the van and we would drive to Tangier, where he would do evening service," she said. "We also had a Christian bookstore in Fez."

Despite her devout upbringing and her distaste for girly-girls, Lynn is a big fan of strip clubs. When she lived in San Francisco, she worked at a bar in the financial district, and one stockbroker in particular kept asking her out. "I was like No, I don't date guys who wear suits. He was like That's the dumbest thing I've ever heard." So they went out for a drink. "I decided I would test this guy," she said. They were at a bar in an area called the Tenderloin, right near the Mitchell Brothers strip club. "It's this world-famous titty bar," said Lynn, excitedly. "It's not even just a titty bar, it's full touch, full nudity, full everything. I love titty bars. I don't know why . . . I'm not attracted to the girls, but I like the bored looks on their faces while they're dancing. They always have those really tacky high-heeled white patent leather pumps on and then they're just staring up at the ceiling. So I'm dragging him from room to room like Check it out! They're fucking! They're having sex! I thought it was hilarious. The guys were kind of desperate looking? And they're just drooling as the girls are going by." Lynn and her date were kicked out of the club that night for making out. "We had sex in the cab on the way home. After that I thought maybe he was kind of okay. So I dated him for three and a half years."

Lynn described the ensuing relationship as "pretty miserable." Despite their bold beginning, they were not a passionate couple. "He's a good-looking guy, but he had gotten really chunky and we didn't have sex for the last year," Lynn said. "That's another thing that I do and I don't know why: If I stop being really attracted to someone, then I can't have sex with them."

Think about the underlying logic of that statement: She doesn't know why she doesn't want to have sex with someone she's not really attracted to. To her, this is a puzzle rather than a question answered. What Lynn is articulating is our baseline assumption that sex is something you should always automatically take when you can get it, something akin to, say, money. The more money, the more sex, the better, because these are things you accumulate to increase your status, your wealth of experience. "I want to get more notches on my belt," as Annie put it; "I want to get to a hundred."

The description all three women offered of their physical experiences sounded less than smoldering. Annie called "this shopping kind of sex" "not that sexual," and characterized her hookups as frequently "mediocre" and "pretty fucking lame." Meg said that "it worked" when she convinced a guy that she'd never been so turned on in her life, but what had she "won"? The dubious privilege of having "antiseptic" sex with someone she was "not that into." (She would have succeeded according to *He's Just Not That Into*

You because she accurately determined that a man was interested in her. But it never occurred to her that the quality of her experience would be compromised because *she* was just not that into *him*.)

Going to a strip club is a similar kind of notch-in-the-belt experience to accumulate, one that will supposedly inspire sex and sexual wildness. But what is Lynn's primary explanation for why she enjoys a "titty bar"? "The bored looks on their faces" when the dancers in "those really tacky high-heeled white patent leather pumps" are "just staring up at the ceiling." That is not a description of arousal, it is a description of barely muffled contempt. Why would you take pleasure in seeing a person wear a compromising costume and watching the tedium of her life unfold? Because you felt she deserved it. Because it was somehow creepily satisfying to see her detached impersonation of wanting, and to see the men's "desperate" response to it. Lynn said she found this "hilarious."

What is the joke?

The entertainment value has to come from people playing out their roles—the "women are beautiful and the men are fools!" as Sheila Nevins put it—but these roles are beyond reductive. "Girls are just girly," Lynn said. "Now I'm like a guy!" Annie felt, in a moment of sexual triumph. But who is this mythological guy we're all trying to be like? Why have we fallen sway to a kind of masculine mystique, determined that to be adventurous is to be like a man, and decided that the best thing we can possibly expect from women is hotness? Even as Annie and Meg and Lynn —three *women*—bravely head out into the night, they still deem this behavior to be like a man's.

Erica Jong's *Fear of Flying*, published in 1973, famously introduced Americans to the idea that a woman might desire a consequence-free "zipless fuck." "I had to create the zipless fuck to rebel against my fifties upbringing," she said. "I told my daughter the other day, 'Your generation does it; my generation just talked about it.' I look at my daughter and her friends in their twenties and they are reveling in their sexuality. They don't feel guilty, and why should they? Men never did. Right now, they're young and beautiful and full of energy and they don't necessarily want to have a relationship, or even necessarily have a guy stay the whole night!

"But I would be happier if my daughter and her friends were crashing through the glass ceiling instead of the sexual ceiling," Jong continued. "Being able to have an orgasm with a man you don't love or having *Sex and the City* on television, that is not liberation. If you start to think about women as if we're all Carrie on *Sex and the City*, well, the problem is: You're not going to elect Carrie to the Senate or to run your company. Let's see the Senate fifty percent female; let's see women in decision-making positions—*that's* power. Sexual freedom can be a smokescreen for how far we *haven't* come."

Unfortunately, I think the situation is worse than

that. Carrie's character had friends, a job, and at least a few other interests besides men and sex. The women who are really being emulated and obsessed over in our culture right now—strippers, porn stars, pinups—*aren't even people*. They are merely sexual personae, erotic dollies from the land of make-believe. In their performances, which is the only capacity in which we see these women we so fetishize, they don't even speak. As far as we know, they have no ideas, no feelings, no political beliefs, no relationships, no past, no future, no *humanity*.

Is this really the best we can do?

Instead of advancing the causes of the women's liberation movement or the sexual revolution, the obdurate prevalence of raunch in the mainstream has diluted the effect of both sex radicals *and* feminists, who've seen their movement's images popularized while their ideals are forgotten. As Candida Royalle said, "We've become a heavily sexualized culture, but it's consumerism and sex rolled into one. Revolutionary movements tend to be co-opted—swallowed up by the mainstream and turned into pop culture. It's a way of neutralizing it, when you think about it . . . it makes it all safe and palatable, it shuts up the radicals. Once that happens, the real power is pretty much dissipated."

Conclusion

The proposition that having the most simplistic, plastic stereotypes of female sexuality constantly reiterated throughout our culture somehow proves that we are sexually liberated and personally empowered has been offered to us, and we have accepted it. But if we think about it, we know this just doesn't make any sense. It's time to stop nodding and smiling uncomfortably as we ignore the crazy feeling in our heads and admit that the emperor has no clothes.

Many women today, whether they are fourteen or forty, seem to have forgotten that sexual power is only one, very specific kind of power. And what's more, looking like a stripper or a Hooters waitress or a Playboy bunny is only one, very specific kind of sexual expression. Is it the one that turns us—*or men*— on the most? We would have to stop endlessly reenacting this one raunchy script in order to find out.

We have to ask ourselves why we are so focused on silent girly-girls in G-strings *faking* lust. This is not a sign of progress, it's a testament to what's still missing from our understanding of human sexuality with all of its complexity and power. We are still so uneasy with the vicissitudes of sex we need to surround ourselves with caricatures of female hotness to safely conjure up the concept "sexy." When you think about it, it's kind of pathetic. Sex is one of the most interesting things we as humans have to play with, and we've reduced it to polyester underpants and implants. We are selling ourselves unbelievably short.

Without a doubt there are *some* women who feel their most sexual with their vaginas waxed, their labia trimmed, their breasts enlarged, and their garments flossy and scant. I am happy for them. I wish them many blissful and lubricious loops around the pole. But there are many other women (and, yes, men) who feel constrained in this environment, who would be happier and feel hotter—more empowered, more sexually liberated, and all the rest of it—if they explored other avenues of expression and entertainment.

This is not a book about the sex industry; it is a

book about what we have decided the sex industry means . . . how we have held it up, cleaned it off, and distorted it. How we depend on it to mark us as an erotic and uninhibited culture at a moment when fear and repression are rampant. In 2004 our forty-second president, George W. Bush, the leader of the free world, proposed an amendment to the U.S. Constitution to forever ban gay marriage—which was *already* illegal. In opinion polls, about 50 percent of this country said they thought Bush had the right idea. If half this country feels so threatened by two people of the same gender being in love and having sex (and, incidentally, enjoying equal protection under the law), that they turn their attention—during *wartime*—to blocking rights already denied to homosexuals, then all the cardio striptease classes in the world aren't going to render us sexually liberated.

As of 2005, federal funding was denied to all public school sex education programs except for those advocating abstinence until marriage. Consequently, a disturbing percentage of young people are equipped with nothing but G-strings and Jenna Jameson to guide them through the roiling sea of hormones they are entering, and all the attendant dangers of STDs and pregnancy that are its sharks. Our national love of porn and pole dancing is not the byproduct of a free and easy society with an earthy acceptance of sex. It is a desperate stab at free-wheeling eroticism in a time and place characterized by intense anxiety. What are we afraid of? Everything . . . which includes sexual freedom and *real* female power.

Women's liberation and empowerment are terms feminists started using to talk about casting off the limitations imposed upon women and demanding equality. We have perverted these words. The freedom to be sexually provocative or promiscuous is not enough freedom; it is not the only "women's issue" worth paying attention to. And we are not even free in the sexual arena. We have simply adopted a new norm, a new role to play: lusty, busty exhibitionist. There are other choices. If we are really going to be sexually liberated, we need to make room for a range of options as wide as the variety of human desire. We need to allow ourselves the freedom to figure out what we internally want from sex instead of mimicking whatever popular culture holds up to us as sexy. *That* would be sexual liberation.

If we believed that we were sexy and funny and competent and smart, we would not need to be like strippers or like men or like anyone other than our own specific, individual selves. That won't be easy, but ultimately it would be no more difficult than the kind of contortions FCPs are constantly performing in an effort to prove themselves. More importantly, the rewards would be the very things Female Chauvinist Pigs want so desperately, the things women deserve: freedom and power.

Afterword

The first person I saw when I arrived for my appearance at the bookstore in Seattle was my spouse's brother Bruce, who is an Evangelical Christian minister. I made a mental note to go easy on the right wing in my talk that evening. Next, I saw my friend Erica, who is a stripper at the famous woman-owned Lusty Lady club. I decided to be (even) more explicit than usual that I don't think there's anything inherently wrong with stripping (or porn for that matter), I think there's something wrong with a culture that equates the selling of sex with sexual liberation. Finally, I saw Lamar Van Dyke. Lamar is a legend in

lesbiandom whom I'd been wanting to meet for a
long time so she could tell me about her adventures
as the head of the Van Dykes, a 1970s lesbian separatist group who smashed monogamy, lived in vans,
didn't eat animals, and didn't speak to men unless
they were waiters or mechanics.

At that point I gave up on catering to my audience.

I'd like to think I was just very smooth, but
really they were very open-minded, and we all ended
up going out for beers after the talk at an enormous
sports bar called The Ram. It was kind of a blast.

That night was a pretty good reflection of my experience with this book in general over the course of
the past year since it's come out: complete dread that
people will hate it eclipsed by fascination if it res-
onates for them—for whatever reason. And the reasons have ranged.

I've received a lot of letters from religious people, which has been great for me because prior to this
correspondence (and, come to think of it, to meeting
Bruce, which happened at about the same time) I
don't think I'd ever come into contact with a strictly
religious person in my entire life. I've learned a lot.
Often, the gist of these letters has been that I make
some good points about the commodification of sexuality, but that I miss the solution: prayer. We agree
to disagree.

To my delight, I've heard from some of the icons
of the feminist movement whom I wrote about in
chapter two. I got to have drinks with Robin Morgan in

her amazing garden. (In New York City, any garden is amazing just for existing, but hers really is nice.) I went to an absolutely rocking Fourth of July party at Susan Brownmiller's apartment. When I was working on the book and begging her to meet with me for an interview (which she never did), Brownmiller regarded me as a total nuisance—and may still—but we definitely had a good time that night. I also got to go on the radio with the feminist and sex radical Susie Bright, whom I didn't write about but now I wish I had.

I've had interactions with quite a few younger women who've read my book as well. The webmaster of oneangrygirl.com sent me an excellent sticker of the mudflapgirl reading the S.C.U.M. Manifesto. Twenty-one-year-old Jessie Wienhold from Toronto, Canada, says, "After reading your book I decided not to get the breast implants I have been planning on getting since I was 17." Jane, a stripper from Sydney, Australia, e-mailed me that "I'm already forcing my boyfriend to read it." And twenty-two-year-old Jennifer Gruselle sent me my favorite letter of all time.

Growing up in suburban Wisconsin, Jennifer "never thought much about feminism or women's rights because I never had to." She was used to being respected for her talents and given a fair shot. Things changed when she joined the Army after graduating from high school. "I found the Army physically challenging, but not impossible," she wrote me. "The military's physical taxation paled in comparison to the strenuous mental decomposition which gradually occurred. And I'm not talking about tough drill sergeants . . . in fact, I considered training a breeze. It was when I got out into the real Army, the real world, for the first time that I realized how substantially my one title of 'female' affected me."

Jennifer was deployed to Baghdad as a medic at the beginning of the Iraq war. "I was attached to an all-male field artillery battalion for the first half of the year and then transferred to an all-male armored battalion for the second half of our tour. Yes, I was the one woman amongst almost five hundred men for 16 months. You would not believe the responses this elicited. When I first arrived, I was sent away. Although I was trained as a medic just like any other male soldier had been, I somehow was not seen as able to do the job."

When it became clear to Jennifer's fellow soldiers that it was either her or no medic at all, "they grudgingly took me back. After a few weeks of wariness, they eventually warmed up to me. I like to think this is because I proved myself time and time again, and showed extreme confidence and competence in many hairy situations. I did not regard myself as special because I was female. I didn't want special treatment or 'protection' from anyone. I carried my own weapon, after all, which I was trained along with all the other male soldiers how to fire. However, these gradual feelings of warmth from my comrades, I learned, did not come entirely from my self-proven ability. They wondered, actually, how I looked out of uniform. In a bikini perhaps. I remember feeling sick even while we were in Iraq as stars like Jessica Simpson paraded around in their bikinis and congratulated all the brave men for being such fearless heroes."

Upon her return to the United States, Jennifer found many of the same dynamics at play. "I didn't feel like a soldier, I felt like a joke. The thing to do when we returned was, of course, frequent every strip club in town," Jennifer said. "My point is, there have been many times over the past few years when I have seriously begun to doubt myself. Maybe I am just being uptight, I thought. But I couldn't ignore that feeling in my head that something was seriously wrong with this whole big picture. I enjoy men, I enjoy sex, I enjoy myself. But I am infuriated every time I drive past a strip club stating 'We've got beer, we've got broads, and we've got booze.' I am even more infuriated when the men—and women—I share my life with want to actually stop and participate. Thanks to your book I will never again question myself."

Of course, not everyone's been so keen on my book or, for that matter, me. One disgruntled reviewer referred to me as "single and childless." (A more accurate description would be coupled and childish.) A guy who came to a reading I did in Boston stood up and yelled at me for fifteen minutes, which I actually found kind of thrilling before the owner of the bookstore told me, "Don't get a big head, he does that to everyone." And then there were the women who run CAKE, who posted a review on my Amazon page in which they suggested I would like to roll back *Roe v. Wade* and put women in the burka. I found their take on my "pure conservatism" pretty creative considering that I explicitly advocate reproductive freedom, the legalization of gay marriage, and comprehensive sexual education in this book and every chance I get. We disagree to disagree. But debate is good for everyone. Besides, I'm not surprised—if you write about sexual politics you're going to piss people off.

What *has* surprised me is how many letters I've gotten from one group in particular: men. They've written because they want to tell me about their granddaughters, or their girlfriends, or because they have commentary on females in general. At first, when people would ask me questions about men and raunch culture, I would say that I had really reported and written a book about women, so I wasn't qualified to respond. But at this point I've received so many letters from men confirming my gut feeling that reducing sexuality to a commercial formula is no better for them than for us, I feel pretty confident in saying so.

The men I've learned the most from are Ted Nordhaus and Michael Shellenberger, who study social values with the group Environics, which sounds to me like the name of a regimen of nutritional supplements but is actually a preeminent market research firm, originally based in Canada. Since 1992 they have been asking a group of 2,500 people questions like "Agree or disagree: Men are naturally superior." The percentage of Americans who agree with that statement has been steadily increasing: between 1992 and 2004 it rose from 42 to 52 percent. The percentage who agree with the statement "father of family must be master in his own house" has likewise risen, from 30 to 40 percent.

What they want to measure is an individual's "core orientation," that is, his or her most deeply held assumptions and ideas, as opposed to passing points of view. So, unlike traditional pollsters, Environics isn't interested in asking questions like "how good a job do you think the president is doing on the economy?" Because the answer to that question might be different, say, the month someone receives a tax refund than it would three months later when that same person is downsized. An individual's answer on a question like that might only represent a "temporal orientation," as Nordhaus puts it, rather than a bedrock belief. But if social values do not change month to month, person to person, they do shift gradually and culturally over time, because younger generations come of age and because societies respond to momentous social change—things like the advent of the women's movement with its enormous impact on women's professional, political, and personal roles. On the next page is a graph that illustrates Environics' findings about the slow motion of American values over roughly the past decade. This is what they call their Map of Social Values.

AUTHORITY

FULFILLMENT

INDIVIDUALITY

SURVIVAL

United States 1992-2004 Sociocultural Trends

Traditional Family
Obedience to Authority
Religiosity
Propriety
National Pride
Primacy of the Family
Everyday Ethics
Work Ethic
Duty
Traditional Gender Identity
Meaningful Moments
American Dream
Spiritual Quest
Selective Use of Professional Services
Effort Toward Health
Social Responsibility
Cultural Assimilation
Consistent Self
Emotional Control
Holistic Health
Discriminating Consumerism
Discerning Hedonism
Social Intimacy
Personal Challenge
Search for Roots
Time Stress
Gender Parity
Personal Expression
Fear of Violence
Concern for Appearance
Civic Engagement
Protection of Privacy
Discount Consumerism
Deconsumption
Patriarchy
Status via Home
Celebrating Passages
Faith in Science
Ethical Consumerism
Introspection & Empathy
American Entitlement
Look Good Feel Good
Aversion to Complexity
Technology Anxiety
Vitality
Strategic Consumption
Sensualism
Mysterious Forces
Confidence in Advertising
Networking
Community Involvement
Heterarchy
Entrepreneurialism
Ecological Concerns
Confidence in Small Business
Adaptive Navigation
Culture Sampling
Brand Apathy
Personal Control
Advertising as Stimulus
Social Mobility
Intuition & Impulse
Parochialism
Need for Uniqueness
Voluntary Simplicity
Laissez-faire
Financial Security
Importance of Spontaneity
Saving on Principal
Attraction for Crowds
Reverse Sexism
Rejection of Order
Personal Escape
Adaptability to Complexity
Skepticism of Advertising
Importance of Brand
Conformity to Norms
Interest in the Unexplained
Personal Creativity
Xenophobia
Joy of Consumption
Modern Racism
More Power for Politics
Global Consciousness
Importance of Aesthetics
Acknowledgement of Racism
Flexible Gender Identity
Sexism
Enthusiasm for New Technology
Religion à la Carte
Rejection of Authority
Confidence in Big Business
Need for Status Recognition
Enthusiasm for Consumption
Multiculturalism
Pursuit of Intensity
Ecological Fatalism
Malleable Self
Buying on Impulse
Fatalism
Ostentatious Consumption
Just Desserts
Active Government
Living Virtually
More Power for Business
Civic Apathy
Equal Relationship with Youth
Everyday Rage
More Power for Media
Flexible Families
Upscale Consumerism
Racial Fusion
Anomie-Aimlessness
Penchant for Risk
Acceptance of Violence
Sexual Permissiveness

2 0 8

To understand the specific ideas represented on the map, have a look at the second chart.

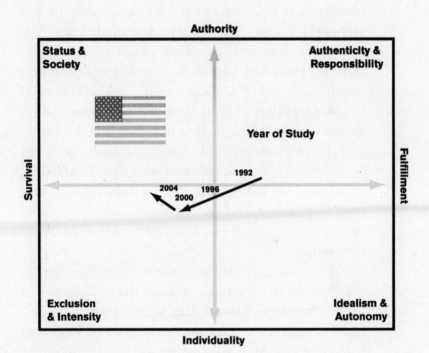

Notice the movement toward the quadrant labeled "Exclusion and Intensity." Within that quadrant are such social values as sexism, racism, more power for business, more power for media, xenophobia, acceptance of violence (which was measured in part by responses to the statement "It's acceptable to use physical force to get something you really want. The important thing is to get what you want."), ostentatious consumption, penchant for risk, and sexual permissiveness, which are some of the values expressed in raunch culture. This is data, not judgment: the responses aren't telling us that if a person is promiscuous he is automatically or necessarily also an SUV-driving white supremacist who likes kickboxing. What they are telling us is that certain social values tend to correlate, and certain social values tend to be incompatible, and these combinations can be counterintuitive.

For example, the movement toward racism is matched by a movement toward the acceptance of multiculturalism. To me, this seems pretty straightforward: change is often accompanied by fear, and fear—fear of losing your power or fear of upsetting people in power—is what fuels racism, sexism, homophobia, and a lot of other bad things. Critics of the Environics research have pointed to (supposedly contradictory) studies that show an increasing acceptance of women in the workplace, but it is entirely possible to recognize or support progress and still harbor anxieties about it. It is possible, for instance, to think of yourself as a smart, competent woman who deserves a promotion and a high salary, and to still feel a need to prove to yourself and others that you can fulfill a sexual stereotype whether it turns you on or not. People do things to get by that are not necessarily the things that would make them feel most content or self-actualized, as we can clearly see in these charts: a move away from "fulfillment" and toward "survival."

Americans are becoming less devoted *both* to traditional values like responsibility and civic engagement *and* to progressive values like gender parity and personal expression. "The values that are showing the strongest growth in America—especially among youth—are the values of the politically disengaged," as Environics founder Michael Adams wrote in his 2005 book *American Backlash*. "What are these values? According to our data, the values showing the most pronounced growth in the United States from 1992 to 2004 fell into three categories: risk-taking and thrill-seeking, Darwinism and exclusion, and consumption and status-seeking." Flashing for "Girls Gone Wild" could be seen as taking a risk, seeking a thrill. The competition among high school girls to see who can concoct that "new way in" to tantalize guys with the help of g-strings and Swiffer mops is a kind of Darwinism, the survival of the skankiest. And shopping for sex, accumulating implants and belt notches, is conspicuous consumption in the hopes of achieving the ultimate in female status: hotness.

AFTERWORD

These are not the progressive values I was raised with, nor are they the traditional values someone like Bruce teaches in his church. I think—I hope—that what has appealed to some people about the book you are holding in your hands is that it espouses something that's fallen out of favor in this country, but is badly needed: idealism.

Notes

Introduction

5 *"When I was in porn"*: Frank Rich, "Finally, Porn Does Prime Time," *New York Times*, July 27, 2003.

5 *"embraced by young women"*: Jennifer Harper, "Buy Playboy for the Articles—Really," *Washington Times*, October 3, 2002.

One. Raunch Culture

An earlier version of the Girls Gone Wild section of this chapter first appeared as dispatches from Miami, Florida, on www.slate.com on March 22, 23, and 24, 2004.

14 *"a public execution"*: www.girlsgonewild.com.

18 *"radical feminists, with our deeper understanding"*: Susan Brownmiller, *In Our Time: Memoir of a Revolution* (Delta, 1999).

NOTES

19 *"I believe that there is a porno-ization"*: 60 Minutes *Wednesday*, CBS, January 5, 2005.

20 *"Strong, powerful women"*: I interviewed Jeff Costa after I sat in on a Cardio Striptease class he taught on March 19, 2003, at a Crunch gym in Los Angeles.

21 *A contestant on* The Bachelor: The fall 2004 season.

22 *"did this for nothing"*: Larry King Live, CNN, May 1, 2004.

22 *Between 1992 and 2004, breast augmentation:* American Society of Plastic Surgeons, www.plasticsurgery.org/public_education/Statistical-Trends.cfm.

22 *"The younger girls think"*: Alex Kuczynski, "A Lovelier You, with Off-the-Shelf Parts," *New York Times*, May 2, 2004.

23 *"The hetero porno antics"*: Simon Doonan, "Simon Says," *New York Observer*, September 22, 2003.

25 *"If that's not being part of the Establishment"*: Alex Kuczynski, "The Sex-Worker Literati," *New York Times*, November 4, 2001.

27 *"who hasn't dreamed"*: Libby Copeland, "Naughty Takes Off," *Washington Post*, November 30, 2003.

29 *No region of the United States:* Jim Holt, "A States' Right Left?" *New York Times Magazine*, November 21, 2004.

29 *In fact, eight of the ten:* Andrew Ward, "South Finds Families That Pray Together May Not Stay Together: Lawmakers Count the Cost of Embarrassingly High Divorce Rates," *Financial Times*, January 24, 2005.

30 *"my boyfriends always tell me"*: Vanessa Grigoriadis, "Princess Paris," *Rolling Stone*, November 19, 2003.

31 *"it was sexy stuff"*: Seymour M. Hersh, "Escape and Evasion," *The New Yorker*, November 12, 2001.

31 *"After Enron, Deregulation Is Looking Less Sexy"*: Kirk Johnson, *New York Times*, February 10, 2002.

31 *"She's a wonderful role model"*: "Driven: Christina Aguilera," VH1, August 6, 2002.

32   *Jay Leno sits floppy faced:* Though Leno has maintained a long lead in the late night ratings, he has also announced that he will turn over *The Tonight Show* to Conan O'Brien in 2009.

32   *her $65 million contract:* Michael Starr, "Matt Gets $5M Less Than Katie," *New York Post,* May 2, 2002.

37   *I went to visit her in Chicago:* I interviewed Christie Hefner, Linda Havard, and Cleo Wilson for about one hour each at the Playboy offices in Chicago on May 8 and 9, 2003.

41   *"Beginning with nude modeling":* Jenna Jameson, *How to Make Love Like a Porn Star: A Cautionary Tale* (Regan Books, 2004).

41   *recruited to be live-in hookers:* Ron Moreau and Michael Hirsh, "Poor Little Rich Kid," *Newsweek,* August 17, 1998.

42   *"When you get yourself into the really contortionist":* "Centerfold Babylon," VH1, October 12, 2003.

42   *"Our job is to go out and bring 'em back":* Ibid.

Two. The Future That Never Happened

46   *"I would like to be in close association":* Mary Cantwell, "The American Woman," *Mademoiselle,* June 1976.

47   *"theatrical bravura":* Susan Brownmiller, *Against Our Will: Men, Women and Rape* (Simon & Schuster, 1975).

47   *"Being good at what was expected of me":* Susan Brownmiller, *Femininity* (Fawcett Columbine, 1984).

48   *"Women as a class":* Susan Brownmiller, "Sisterhood Is Powerful: A Member of the Women's Liberation Movement Explains What It's All About," *New York Times Magazine,* March 15, 1970.

49   *"Background, education, ideology":* Todd Gitlin, *The Sixties: Years of Hope, Days of Rage* (Bantam, 1987).

49   *"The position of women in SNCC":* I've heard Stokely Carmichael's infamous quote reiterated in various, slightly different formulations (which always include

the words "position," "women," and "prone"). The phrasing I quote here is the most common, cited by both Gitlin in *The Sixties* and Brownmiller in *In Our Time*.

49 *"Friedan, the mother of the movement":* Brownmiller, "Sisterhood Is Powerful."

50 *"The momentum was extraordinary":* Telephone interviews with Susan Brownmiller, January 2001 and January 2004 and several subsequent e-mails.

51 *"I was committed to being a part":* Ayers was quoted in Sam Green and Bill Siegel's remarkable film *The Weather Underground* (Docurama, 2003), for which the documentarians interviewed everyone from Don Strickland, the FBI agent assigned to stalk the Weathermen, to Kathleen Cleaver, a former member of the Black Panther party and the wife of Panther Eldridge Cleaver.

51 *"We served a mix of Italian":* Telephone interview with Dolores Alexander, December 1, 2003.

52 *"It was more than jubilant":* Telephone interview with Jill Ward, December 13, 2003.

54 *Hite distributed 100,000 questionnaires:* Shere Hite, *The Hite Report: A Nationwide Study of Female Sexuality* (Dell, 1976).

55 *"our ferocious antisexuality":* Oriana Fallaci, "I Am in the Center of the World," *Look,* January 10, 1967.

56 *"I was a feminist before":* Wil S. Hylton, "What I've Learned," *Esquire,* June 2002.

57 *"rather alienating and dull":* Lisa Eisner and Roman Alonso, "An Eye for the Ladies," *New York Times Magazine,* March 30, 2003.57

57 *"The rabbit, the bunny, in America":* Fallaci, "I Am in the Center of the World."

59 *"If you're somebody's sister":* Hugh M. Hefner, "Introduction," *Playboy,* December 1953.

60 *"Women were the major beneficiary":* Hylton, "What I've Learned."

60 *"at a loss for words": Inside Deep Throat* (film), Fenton Bailey and Randy Barbato (Universal, 2005).

64 *"I looked at pornography":* Michael Moorcock, "Fighting Talk," *New Statesman & Society,* April 21, 1995.

65 *"Suddenly, pornography became the enemy":* Interview with Candida Royalle, New York City, December 1, 2003.

65 *"[I]f one's sexual experience has always":* Andrea Dworkin, *Intercourse* (Free Press, 1997).

66 *"Bill Clinton's fixation on oral sex":* Andrea Dworkin, "Dear Bill and Hillary," *The Guardian* (London), January 29, 1998.

70 *"The new sexual revolution is":* www.cakenyc.com/index nav.html as of March 23, 2005.

70 *"gooey, sweet, yummy":* 20/20, ABC, February 20, 2004.

71 *perceived weaknesses of* Sex and the City: They write, for instance, "moving on to a [2004] episode of *Sex and the City,* women were treated to a rather unhealthy dose of what we like to call 'Have your CAKE, but don't eat it too.' Samantha is told (by a male physician) that her breast cancer could be caused by the fact that she has not had any children—swiftly invoking the age-old idea that being sexually active without reproductive intentions may be threatening to your health. Unfortunately, the message ended there and did not in any way explain why, how, or if there is an increased chance of having breast cancer if a woman does not bear children. Moreover, what could have been a great opportunity to make a positive statement about women and their sexual choices quickly dissolved into a reactionary response." I think they're being weirdly literal here. The whole point of the episode was that being diagnosed with cancer is a shocking, destabilizing experience, so the character Samantha bolted from her male physician's office before he could explain anything or offer any positive statements about women and their sexual choices,

telling him, "You're lucky to have touched my breasts!"

71 *the front page of the* New York Post: John Lehmann, "Inside the Freak Box," *New York Post,* June 12, 2001.

71 *"CAKE Underground":* October 3, 2003

74 *"serious sisters of the sixties":* Jennifer Baumgardner and Amy Richards, *Manifesta: Young Women, Feminism, and the Future* (Farrar, Straus and Giroux, 2000).

76 *"I was standing in the shower":* I interviewed Erica Jong on the telephone on February 15, 2002, and we spoke again in person after an event at the 92nd Street YMHA on November 4, 2003, in celebration of the thirtieth anniversary of *Fear of Flying.*

79 Maxim *magazine's "Hot 100":* June 11, 2003.

81 *"you try getting 800 people":* Virginia Vitzthum, "Stripped of Our Senses," *Elle,* December 2003.

83 *"They kicked Betty upstairs":* Telephone interview with Jacqui Ceballos, January 2004.

Three. Female Chauvinist Pigs

Selections from this chapter originally appeared in the article "Female Chauvinist Pigs," *New York* magazine, January 22, 2001, including my interviews with Sherry, Anyssa, and Rachel and my visit to the set of *The Man Show.*

89 *On the first warm day:* The New York Women in Film & Television brunch for Sheila Nevins was held at The Society of Illustrators in New York on May 31, 2000.

90 *She was once profiled:* Nell Casey, "The 25 Smartest Women in America," *Mirabella,* September 1999.

90 *"a revered player":* "New York's 100 Most Influential Women in Business," *Crain's New York Business,* September 27–October 3, 1999.

94 *In 2003, women held:* This information comes from Dr. Martha M. Lauzen, a professor at San Diego State University's School of Communications, who has conducted studies of both the film and television industries annually for the past decade.

NOTES

95   *"I think really that your desire":* Nancy Milford, *Savage Beauty: The Life of Edna St. Vincent Millay* (Random House, 2001).

95   *"from behind":* Gail Sheehy, "Flying Solo," *Vanity Fair,* August 2001.

95   *"masculine kind of independence":* Carl Rollyson and Lisa Paddock, *Susan Sontag: The Making of an Icon* (Norton, 2000).

95   *"I have the biggest cock in the building!":* Judith Newman, "The Devil and Miss Regan," *Vanity Fair,* January 2005.

100   *Erin Eisenberg, a city arts administrator, and her little sister Shaina:* I met with the Eisenbergs at their parents' apartment in New York City on October 8, 2001.

102   *"My best mentors and teachers":* Carrie Gerlach e-mailed a letter to the editor on January 30, 2001 in response to my *New York* magazine article "Female Chauvinist Pigs."

104   *"the wrongheadedness, distortions and wishful thinkings":* J. C. Furnas, *Goodbye to Uncle Tom* (William Sloane Associates, 1956).

104   *"a Spanish gentleman":* Harriet Beecher Stowe, *Uncle Tom's Cabin* (Norton Critical Editions, 1994).

104   *"in all other respects as white":* James Baldwin, "Everybody's Protest Novel," *Partisan Review* 16, June 1949.

106   *"theatrical industry called 'Tomming'":* Mary C. Henderson and Joseph Papp, *Theater in America* (Abrams, 1986).

108   *"if civilization had been left in female hands":* Camille Paglia, *Sexual Personae: Art and Decadence from Nefertiti to Emily Dickinson* (Yale University Press, 1990).

109   *"They have this stupid, pathetic":* Camille Paglia, *Sex, Art, and American Culture* (Vintage, 1992).

111   *"even made teeny-weeny bikinis":* Mary Wells Lawrence, *A Big Life (in Advertising)* (Knopf, 2002).

111   *"Mary Wells Uncle Tommed it":* Steinem made the comment on the local television news in Dallas, Texas. Wells

Lawrence printed an account of her reaction in her memoir (ibid).

Four. From Womyn to Bois

Selections from this chapter previously appeared in the article "Where the Bois Are," *New York* magazine, January 12, 2004.

120 *"a woman without a man"*: this sardonicism—which was put on bumper stickers, T-shirts, and buttons in the seventies—is usually attributed to Gloria Steinem. It was actually coined in 1970 by Irina Dunn, an Australian politician and journalist whose phrasing was "a woman needs a man like a fish needs a bicycle," a play on "Man needs God like a fish needs a bicycle."

120 *"Lesbianism is a women's liberation plot"*: According to Susan Brownmiller's account in *In Our Time*, the Radicalesbians shut off the lights at the Second Congress to Unite Women in May 1970, which was held at a school in Manhattan. When they turned the lights back on, members of their group wearing LAVENDER MENACE T-shirts were onstage and posters that proclaimed "TAKE A LESBIAN TO LUNCH" and "WE ARE ALL LESBIANS" lined the room.

120 *The first installment of* The Furies: Ginny Berson and Charlotte Bunch, *The Furies*, January 1972.

121 *"I never really wanted to grow up"*: Interview with Lissa Doty at the Lexington Club, San Francisco, September 19, 2003.

122 *"I think non-monogamy is a part"*: Interview with Sienna, Brooklyn, New York, September 8, 2003.

124 *"It's just wild to me"*: Telephone interview with Deb Schwartz, October 10, 2003.

126 *"I'm so against the whole butch-femme"*: Interview with Julien Rosskam, Brooklyn, New York, September 10, 2003.

NOTES

127 *"I've noticed a lot of different levels"*: e-mail from Ian sent on August 4, 2003. Our conversation in Brooklyn, New York, took place on August 23, 2003.

131 *she had met "maybe thirty"*: I interviewed Sarah at my apartment in New York City on August 24, 2003.

132 *On a warm fall night, Diana Cage*: I interviewed Diana Cage and her friends at the Lexington Club in San Francisco on September 18, 2003. I accompanied Gibson to Club Galia in San Francisco on September 19, 2003.

Five. Pigs in Training

140 *In December 2002*: Emma Stickgold, "Sexual Incident Reported on Silver Lake School Bus," *Boston Globe*, March 26, 2004.

140 *1999 in Talbot County*: Laura Sessions Stepp, "Parents Are Alarmed by an Unsettling New Fad in Middle Schools: Oral Sex," *Washington Post*, July 8, 1999.

140 *two thirteen-year-olds in Beaver County: The Oprah Winfrey Show*, Harpo Productions, Inc., March 25, 2004.

140 *an eighth-grade girl at Horace Mann*: Daphne Merkin, "The Paris Hilton Effect," *New York* magazine, May 10, 2004.

141 *senior at Manhattan's Trinity School*: I spoke with students from the New York City schools Trinity, Fieldston, Horace Mann, and Saint Ann's in June 2004.

143 *"I don't care if a baby"*: Laura Sessions Stepp, "Playboy's Bunny Hops Into Teens' Closets: Sexist Symbol of '60s Now a Hot Seller," *Washington Post*, June 17, 2003.

145 *"i love their style"*: e-mails from Jessica received August 6, 2004.

147 *"Plus I have a really great schedule"*: Interview with David at the Royal Ground Coffee House & Art Gallery, Oakland, California, September 1, 2004.

150 *"Definitely girls hook up"*: Interview with Anne at Jamba Juice, Oakland, California, September 6, 2004.

150 *"always the biggest dork":* Interview with Robin, Berkeley, California, September 7, 2004.

156 *"in the many hundreds of studies":* Deborah L. Tolman, *Dilemmas of Desire: Teenage Girls Talk About Sexuality* (Harvard University Press, 2002).

160 *"The majority of high school students":* According to the CDC's 2001 Youth Risk Behavior Survey, 60.5 percent of twelfth graders have had sexual intercourse.

160 *Eighty percent of Americans:* Sexual Information and Education Clearinghouse of the United States.

161 *According to the Alan Guttmacher Institute:* Teenagers' Sexual and Reproductive Health: Developed Countries, www.agi-usa.org/pubs/fb_teens.html.

163 *"voluntary but unwanted":* 2003 National Survey of Adolescents and Young Adults: Sexual Health Knowledge, Attitudes and Experiences, The Henry J. Kaiser Family Foundation, www.kff.org/youthhivstds/3218-index.cfm.

169 *The April 2005 issue:* "Harper's Index," *Harper's* magazine, April 2005.

Six. Shopping for Sex
171 *"This is not how women talk":* Ann Coulter, reprinted in *How to Talk to a Liberal (If You Must)* (Crown Forum, 2004).

172 *a feathery pair of mules:* "I Heart NY," *Sex and the City,* Season 4, Episode 66.

172 *Another episode was devoted:* "A Woman's Right to Shoes," Season 6, Episode 83.

173 *"I don't believe in the Republican party":* "Politically Erect," Season 3, Episode 32.

173 *A do-gooder asked if Carrie:* "Attack of the Five Foot Ten Woman," Season 3, Episode 33.

175 *"should be on every woman's night table":* The Oprah Winfrey Show, Harpo Productions, Inc., September 22, 2004.

176 *On the occasion of the thirtieth:* "Sex and What Women

Want Now," 92nd Street YMHA, New York, June 17, 2003.

177 *"interviewed over three thousand women"*: Pearlstein was rounding up. The Center for the Advancement of Women commissioned the Princeton Survey Research Associates, Inc., who interviewed 2,329 women for their 2001 report "Progress and Perils: How Gender Issues Unite and Divide Women."

178 *"The fantasy of the porn star"*: Timothy Greenfield-Sanders, *Thinking XXX* (HBO Films, 2004).

178 *between $8 billion and $15 billion:* Joshua Kurlantzick, "Strip Club's Cover Charge Is Voter Registration Card," *New York Times*, October 5, 2004.

181 *presented to the American Psychological Association:* Abigail Zuger, "Many Prostitutes Suffer Combat Disorder, Study Finds," *New York Times*, August 18, 1998.

181 *"Pornography is a specific form"*: Melissa Farley, Preface, *Prostitution, Trafficking, and Traumatic Stress* (Haworth Maltreatment & Trauma Press, 2003).

187 *"I literally have thoughts like"*: Interview with Annie at her home in Massachusetts, August 4, 2004.

189 *"I hooked up with this guy in Vegas"*: Interview with Meg at the Standard Hotel, Los Angeles, February 16, 2002.

190 *"The great thing about Miami"*: Interview with Lynn Frailey, Miami, April 11, 2003.

Conclusion

199 *which was* already *illegal:* The gay marriage certificates issued in Massachusetts are not actually substantive, because they can't offer crucial federal benefits like Social Security, parental rights, or inheritance protection, which we consider central to the institution of marriage.

199 *In opinion polls:* According to Gallup polls in which people were asked "Would you favor or oppose a constitutional amendment that would define marriage as being

between a man and a woman, thus barring marriages between gay or lesbian couples?" the percentage of respondents who answered in favor was 50 percent in July 2003, 53 percent in February 2004, and 50 percent in March 2004. In the November 2004 election, ballot measures banning same-sex marriage and/or civil unions passed overwhelmingly in eleven states.

Acknowledgments

First, thanks to Dan Conaway for making this book happen.

I would also like to thank my talented editor Liz Stein for believing in this book, my agent Lane Zachary for believing in me, and my fact checker Yael Kohen for believing in due diligence. Thanks to Nicole Kalian and Dominick Anfuso at Free Press for the great gift of their enthusiasm.

John Homans has been my friend and editor at *New York* magazine for eight years. We worked together on the article "Female Chauvinist Pigs" on which this book is based. He and Adam Moss, our editor-in-chief, were both gracious and supportive while I periodically disappeared to write this book. Working with them is deeply rewarding and, more often than not, a lot of fun.

Amanda Fortini and Susan Dominus shared their insights with me and helped me to think about things in new ways. My former professors Joel Pfister, Richard Slotkin, and Khachig Tololyan generously held my hand through the research and writing of the Uncle Tom section. I am also extremely grateful to the following people for their favors, ideas, and encouragement throughout this process: Jesse Blockton, Kristina Dechter, Michael Goff, Isabel Gonzalez, Dee Dee Gordon, Vanessa Grigoriadis, Matt Hyams, Meredith Kahn, David Klagsbrun, Erika Malm, Craig Marks, Caroline Miller, Emily Nussbaum, Maer Roshan, René Steinke, Ahna Tessler, Jennie Thompson, Jennifer Wachtell, and Elisa Zonana. Special thanks to Emma Jemima Jacobson-Sive for a decade and counting of friendship and inspiration, and to M, whose talents as a writer and editor are exceeded only by his talents as a matchmaker.

Finally, thanks to Amy Norquist, for everything.

Index

Index

Index

Index

Index

Index

Victoria's Secret, 20, 21, 99
Vidal, Gore, 25
Vietnam War, 50
Virginity, 160
Vulva, plastic surgery of, 23

Wallace, Mike, 32
Walters, Barbara, 28
Ward, Jill, 51, 52, 84
Warhol, Andy, 88
Washington, Denzel, 80
Washington Post, 26–27, 143
Wattleton, Faye, 176–178,
    184–185
Waxman, Henry, 157
Weathermen, 51
Weissman, Hope, 77
Wells Lawrence, Mary,
    110–111
Wesleyan University, 3, 76–78
Wharton, Edith, vii
Who Wants to Marry a Mil-

lionaire? (television
    show), 21
Williams, Vanessa, 27
Wilson, Cleo, 35
Winfrey, Oprah, 26, 175
Woman Hating (Dworkin), 63
Women Against Pornography,
    18, 60–61
Women's liberation move-
    ment, 46–55, 57, 60–70,
    74, 75, 82–88, 196, 200
Women's Strike for Equality
    (1970), 82–85
Worley, Mike, 158–159

Xena the Warrior Princess
    (television show), 75
XXX: 30 Porn-Star Portraits
    (Greenfield-Sanders),
    25, 178

Yale University, 85

About the Author

ARIEL LEVY is a contributing editor at *New York* magazine, where she writes about sexuality, culture, and gender politics. Her work has also appeared in *Slate, Vogue, The Washington Post, The Guardian* (London), and *The New York Times*.